PENGUINS, PINEAPPLES
& PANGOLINS

PENGUINS, PINEAPPLES & PANGOLINS

First Encounters with the Exotic

CLAIRE COCK-STARKEY

CONTENTS

PEOPLE, PLACES & CUSTOMS 141

INTRODUCTION

Yet true it is, that according to the marvailes of the World, and differences which natural things have in divers Regions under Heaven, and divers constellations of the same, under which they are created, wee see that some such Plants and Herbes as are hurtful in one Countrie, are harmless and wholesome in other Regions. And Birds which in one Province are of good taste, are in others so unsavoury that they may not bee eaten. Men likewise in some Countries are blacke, are in other places white: and yet are both these and they, men.

Samuel Purchas (c. 1577–1626). *Purchas his Pilgrimage or Relations of the World* (1613)

In an age when 'just Google it' has become a stock phrase, it can seem as if all information is but a click away. We have become so accustomed to knowing, that the sense of awe and excitement from that moment of discovery has been lost – everything has become ordinary to us. But if we travel back in time just a few hundred years, before the age of globalisation, Europeans were encountering extraordinary new foods, animals, plants, peoples and cultures for the first time as overseas trade routes opened up. Samuel Purchas's ponderings in *Purchas his Pilgrimage or Relations of the World* (1613) offer us a glimpse into the mind of someone discovering the diverse marvels of the world for the first time. It is this wide-eyed wonder that *Penguins, Pineapples & Pangolins* captures by inviting the reader to cast off their modern omniscience and return to a simpler time, when the world was full of undiscovered delights.

Humans have always searched out new experiences and this has fuelled exploration. The early Polynesians set out in outrigger canoes, the Vikings used rather larger ships to discover new lands and the Romans were inspired to explore in order to expand their empire. From the fifteenth to the seventeenth century the European powers set sail to find new lands and set up trade routes. It is from this era, known as the Age of Exploration, that most of the accounts in this book come.

As the Dutch, Spanish, Portuguese and English set out to explore new lands, motivated by the race to control the commodities of the New World, the merchant-adventurers were constantly exposed to new experiences. Thankfully, many recorded and published their accounts for the public back at home, which was thirsty for information on these strange new lands.

The books I consulted in my research, and from which I have used extracts, were written by a mixed cast of characters, spanning in time from the Middle Ages up to the twentieth century. They range from English privateers (some might say pirates) such as Captain William Dampier (1651–1715), reformed convicts such as George Barrington (1755–1804), and Flemish missionaries such as William of Rubruck (1220–1293), to unfortunate victims of kidnap such as Andrew Battell (1565–1614). This provides a range of voices, from the barely literate, recounting their tale for another to publish on their behalf, to highly educated naturalists providing their own expert analysis of the sights they beheld.

The experiences include seeing a shark (and also suffering the results of getting too close to a shark), observing bats five times the size of those found at home, drinking coffee, eating a banana, catching sight of the monolithic Easter Island statues, witnessing a tattooed person and being terrified by strange fish in the sea. The explorers frequently have no idea what they are describing, and at times do not yet have a word or a name to give the animal, food or object they are encountering.

It is fascinating to see these adventurers use their limited frame of reference to try and describe the wonders they are seeing. It is unsurprising that the taste of a new fruit is frequently compared to that of an apricot, the size of a tree is often given in relation to a pear tree and animals are described as 'of the bigness of a [insert native European animal here]'. Many of the explorers had also endured long and perilous sea voyages and so their priority on reaching land was not admiring local nature but eating local nature.

We can only imagine what it must have been like to see exotic animals, taste new foods and experience strange cultures for the very first time. These adventurers were exploring the world during a period when most people rarely travelled farther than their nearest market town, ate a limited diet of seasonal food and lived within a rigid class system and a fairly homogeneous culture.

Some of the extracts collected here provide us with the first ever European description of an animal or plant, so it is inevitable that at times the travellers make false assumptions or rather strange claims, but this is part of the joy in reading these early accounts – getting inside the mind of someone who is having a fresh experience with something for which there is no encyclopedia entry.

It is this wonderment that I hope I have captured. I have tried to let the voices of the intrepid explorers speak for themselves. Therefore some extracts are reproduced verbatim, with the original archaic or phonetic spelling and punctuation (though I have at times added modern spellings where the meaning is unclear). Some extracts have been translated from their original language and have been tidied up grammatically.

So why not jettison the weight of modern knowledge and allow *Penguins, Pineapples & Pangolins* to gift us the opportunity of listening to the voices of European pioneers, and let us join in marvelling at the wonders of the world?

ANIMALS & BIRDS

Giraffe

Giraffes have been known in Europe since Roman times. In 46 BC Julius Caesar brought back to Rome a large menagerie of exotic animals, including a giraffe, to celebrate his successes in Egypt. The Romans, puzzled by the giraffe's seeming likeness to both the camel and the leopard, gave it the portmanteau name 'cameleopard'.

Many people flocked to see the amazing animal and Julius Caesar, keen to capitalise on this spectacle, had the poor beast ripped to pieces by lions in the arena. Hundreds of years later, in 1486, another giraffe was sent to Italy, this time to the hugely influential Lorenzo de' Medici. It is unclear who gifted the giraffe but it is possible that it was one of the Sultans of Egypt, keen to forge ties with the powerful Italian family.

The giraffe became known as the Medici giraffe and such was its impact on Florentine society that it soon appeared in frescoes, poetry and contemporary paintings, such as Domenico Ghirlandaio's *The Adoration of the Magi* (1488). Unfortunately the giraffe was not to last long. It broke its neck after getting its head caught in the roof of the stables.

The following description of a giraffe comes from *Purchas his Pilgrimage* (1613) by Samuel Purchas,[1] in which the author collected travellers' tales from the Elizabethan and Jacobean eras:

---

[1] Despite publishing extensive tomes on travel and exploration, Purchas himself never even left England, confessing that he had never been '200 miles from *Thaxted* in *Essex* where I was borne.'

Many are the creatures which Africa yieldeth, not usuall in our parts. Elephants are there in plenty, and keepe in great herds together. The Giraffa, or Camelopardalis; a beast not often seene, yet very tame, and of a strange composition, mixed of a Libard [leopard], Hart, Buffe and Camell, and by reason of his long legs before, and shorter behind, not able to graze without difficultie, but with his high head, which he can stretch forth halfe a pikes length in height, feeds on leaves and boughs of trees.

After the sad demise of the Medici giraffe, a living example was not seen in Europe again until 1827, when Ottoman commander Mehmet Ali Pasha sent three giraffes: one for King George IV, one for Charles X of France and one for the Austrian Emperor, Francis II. Only Zarafa, the giraffe of Charles X, survived more than a few years. She lived in Paris's Jardin des Plantes for eighteen years and was much admired until her death, when she was stuffed; and she is now on display in the museum of La Rochelle.

Macaw

A New Voyage and Description of the Isthmus of America (1699) by Lionel Wafer (1640–1705) includes this lovely depiction of the macaw:

Macaw-birds are here also in good plenty. 'Tis shap'd not much unlike a Parrot, but is as large again as the biggest of them. It has a Bill like a Hawk's; and a bushy Tail, with two or three long straggling Feathers, all Red or Blue: The Feathers all over the body are of several very bright and lovely Colours, Blue, Green and Red. The Pinions of the Wings of Some of them are all Red, of others all Blue, and the Beaks yellow. They make a great Noise in a Morning, very hoarse and deep, like Men who speak much in the Throat. The Indians keep these Birds tame, as we do Parrots or Mag-pies: But after they have kept them close some time, and taught them to speak some Words in their Language, they suffer them to go abroad in the Day-time into the Woods, among the wild ones; from whence they will on their own accord return in the Evening to the Indian's Houses or Plantations, and give notice of their arrival by their fluttering and prating. They will exactly imitate the Indians Voices, and their way of Singing, and they will call the Chicaly-Chicaly in its own Notes, as exactly as the Indians themselves, whom I have observ'd to be very expert at it. 'Tis the most beautiful and pleasant Bird that ever I saw; and the Flesh is sweet-tasted enough, but black and tough.

Crocodile & alligator

Richard Blome (1635–1705) offers up a classic description of an alligator in his 1678 *Description of the Island of Jamaica*:

> *In many of the River and Land-Ponds, are Alligators, which are very voracious Creatures, yet seldome do they prey upon a Man, as being very easie to be avoided, for he can only move forwards, and that he doth with great swiftness, and strength and is as slow in turning. Some are 10, 15 or 20 foot long, their backs are scaly and impenetrable, so that they are hardly to be killed, except in the Belly or Eye. They have four Feet or Finns with which they go or swim. They are observed to make no kind of Noise: and the usual course for the getting their prey, is to lie on the banks of Rivers, and as any beast or fowl cometh to drink, they suddenly seize on them; and the rather, for that they do so much resemble a long peece of dry wood, or some dead thing.*

That crocodiles were formidable beasts seems to have been quickly recognised by early explorers. Aristocratic adventurer Sir Thomas Herbert (1606–1682) first published *Some Years Travels into Africa & Asia* in 1634. Herbert came across crocodiles on the Indonesian island of Sumatra and was amazed by their size and ferocity:

The rivers flow with fish and might prove more delightful for the Net and Angle, did not those hateful Crocodiles frustrate both ... seeing these Amphibii are observed to be one of the greatest wonders we meet with, in that from so small a beginning as an Egg not much bigger than that of a Turkie it increases to eight or ten yards in length: and whereas all other creatures have their growth unto a period and then decay, the Crocodile only grows bigger and bigger until its death. Their bodies are not longer than their tail, a weapon of like use with them the proboscis is to the Elephant: Their mouth is very wide, at one gulp being able to swallow horse or man; their teeth are ingrailed; have no tongue; cannot move the upper jaw: and albeit the belly be penetrable the back is hardly to be pierced.

Naturalists were fascinated by the many different types of crocodile found around the world; here George Edwards (1694–1773) in his posthumously published 1776 book *Some Memoirs of the Life and Works of George Edwards* describes how some dead gharials (river-dwelling crocodiles native to India) were transported back to London:

The Narrow Beak'd Crocodile of the Ganges, with an open belly. Three of these crocodiles were sent from Bengal about the year 1747, to the late Dr. Mead, physician in ordinary to the King; two of which he preserved in his collection, and presented the third to the late curious Mrs. Kennon, and since the decease of these worthy persons, they became the property of Mr. James Lemon of London, who obliged Mr. Edwards with one of them to produce to the Royal Society.

The narrowness of the beaks is the most extraordinary circumstance in this crocodile, which appears like the bill of the bird called Gooseander. It has small sharp teeth. Another peculiarity is a paunch, or open purse, in the middle of the underside of the belly, which seems to be naturally formed with round hips, and a hollow within, perhaps to receive its young in the time of danger; as it appears in the American animal, called an Opossum. Dr. Parsons gave it as his opinion, that the opening in the belly was really natural, it having no appearance of being cut or torn open. In other respects, it hath all the marks common to Allegators and Crocodiles, viz. particular strong, square scales on the back, which in the young ones appear distinct and regular, but in the old ones lose their distinct form, and become knobbed and rough, like the bark of an old tree.

Despite the confidence with which Mr Edwards claims this 'pouch' in the crocodile's belly is for carrying its babies I can find no evidence to support the existence of such a pouch. Another explorer to make some false assumptions about the crocodile was Dr John Francis Gemelli Careri (1651–1725). Gemelli Careri was an Italian adventurer who financed his five-year trip round the world by buying and selling goods on his travels. Despite being a well-educated lawyer his knowledge of natural history was somewhat lacking, as this description from *A Voyage Round the World* (1700) of the crocodiles he encountered in the Philippines attests:

As for the Crocodils Providence has signaliz'd it self after several manners in them. For in the first place the Females of these Monsters being extraordinary Fruitful, so as to bring sometimes 50 Crocodils, the Rivers and Lakes would have been full of them in a very short time, to the great damage of Mankind, had not Nature caus'd it to lye in wait where the young ones are to pass, and swallow them down one by one; so that only those few escape that take another way. Secondly, the Crocodils have no passage for Excrements,[2] but only Vomit the small Matter that remains in their stomachs after Digestion. Thus the Meat continues there a long time, and the Creature is not hungry every Day; which if they were, they could not be fed without the utter Ruin of infinite Men and Beasts. Some of them being open'd there have been found in their Bellies Mens Bones and Skuls, and Stones, which the Indians say they swallow to pave their Stomach.

It seems travellers mainly saw crocodiles as a pest due to the danger they posed both to the fish and the fisherman. Dutchman

---

2 Happily I can confirm crocodiles can and do poo.

Christopher Fryke (b. 1659) in his 1700 account of his travels in Indonesia *A Relation of Two Several Voyages made into the East Indies* was keen to beat the crocodiles at their own game:

The Rivers thereabouts are much pestered with Crocodiles. While I was there we used to go a walking in Evenings, we observed one of them for several nights that used to run out of the hedge into the River, as soon as it spied or heard us coming towards him: Upon which a desire took us to try and catch him if we could; which we did in this manner.

We took a long Rope, to which we fastened a strong double Hook, full of beards: And instead of arming it with wires, we did it with Pack-thread; which being loose about it, get in between its Teeth, and hinders him from snapping the Hook off: This done, we tyed a Dog to this with the Hook under his belly: And setting him upon a Board, thrust him out into the River, and fasten'd the Cord to a Tree: Quickly after, the Dog fell a barking and howling, and the Crocodile did not fail to come to him; and very greedily swallowed him in: Upon which the Hook struck into his

Throat, and had him fast. We had so good success with this, that we after-
wards caught a great many of them. The biggest we caught was twenty
seven foot long; and when we opened it, we found two Steen-Bockiens[3],
and the head of a black Boy in his belly.

Likewise, John (or Jean) Mocquet (1575–1617), French traveller, who encountered crocodiles in the West Indies, offered up an
account in *Travels and Voyages into Africa, Asia and America, the East*
and West-Indies; Syria, Jerusalem and the Holy-Land (1696) that would
be familiar to many hungry adventurers:

I made the Dissection of a Crocodile, and Eat some of it's flesh, which
is pretty good only it is a little sweet and unsavoury though I had well
Salted and Spiced it.

Lionel Wafer in his 1699 *A New Voyage and Description of the*
Isthmus of America was also something of a connoisseur when it
came to eating reptiles:

Alligator's and Guano's [iguana?], which are also very good Meat,
especially the Tail of the Alligator, I have eaten in several Parts of
the West-Indies; but I don't remember my seeing either of them in the
Isthmus. The Guano is all over very good Meat, prefer'd to a Pullet or
Chicken, either for the Meat or Broth. Their Eggs also are very good; but
those of the Alligator have too much of a musky Flavour, and sometimes
smell very strong of it.

---

3 The writer later describes these animals thus: 'a sort of creature they call
Steen-Bockiens, which is made much like a Hare, and differs only in that it hath
small Horns, and the Meat of 'em is far more delicate'. This could be a Muntjac deer.

Penguin

The Embassy of Sir Thomas Roe to the Court of the Great Mogul 1615–1619 contains this account of a penguin observed in the Cape of Good Hope and which brought to the author's mind Plato's Latinised description of the human race:

> *On Pengwyn there is a foule soe Called that goes upright, his winges without feathers hanging downe like sleves faced with whyte; they fley not but walk in Pathes and keepe their divisions and quarters orderly; they are a strange fowle or rather a Miscelanius creation of beast, bird and Fishe, but most of bird, confuting that difinition of man to be Animall bipes impluna [that unfeathered two-legged thing], which is nearer a description of this Creature.*

Peter Mundy (*c.* 1600–1667) in *The Travels of Peter Mundy in Europe and Asia 1608–1667* (1667) was somewhat in awe of the penguins he

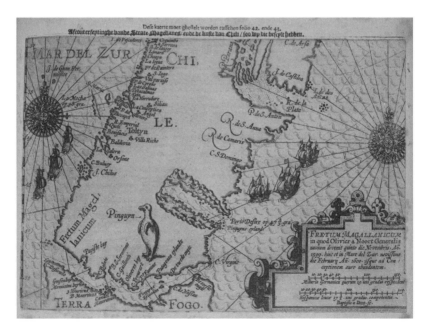

came across in South Africa. They must have seemed unlike any bird he had seen before. Naturally they were not so exceptional as to prevent him from eating them:

Penguins is a kinde of Fowle that cannot flye att all, haveing resemblance of Wyngs which hang downe like sleeves, with which, as with Finns, hee swimmeth exceeding swifte. They live on Fish. Hee breedeth on the land, makeing his Neste in holes under low bushes and shrubbs. They are easily taken, not being able to flye nor runne, only bite a little to noe purpose, bodied like a Ducke but much bigger, head and bill, like a Gull, walkinge and goeinge almost upright, blacke on the Back, white under the belly, which cometh to their head round over their Eyes with a stroake that Thwarts over their breaste ... They taste somewhat fishey. I am also somewhat the learger on this Fowle, because theis are much spoken of, and seemeing verie strange to mee.

Sir Thomas Herbert also encountered some penguins in South Africa and recorded his (very similar) impressions in *Some Years Travels into Africa & Asia* (1677, 4th ed.):

[We] dropt our Anchor 14 Leagues short of Souldania bay afore a small isle call'd Coney-Isle through corruption of speech, the proper name for the isle being Cain yne in Welch. The isle is three miles about, in which we saw an abundance of pen-gwins, in Welch White-heads agreeable to their colour; a Bird that of all other goes most erect in its motion, the wings or fins hanging down like sleeves, covered with down instead of Feathers, their legs serving them better than their wings; they feed on fish at Sea and grass ashore, and have holes to live in like Conies; a degenerate Duck, for using both sea and shore, it feeds in the one, breeds in the other; is very fat and oily, and some adventure to eat them.

Captain William Dampier (1651–1715) in *A New Voyage Round the World* (1699) saw a number of penguins on his travels across the South Seas and, like Peter Mundy and Sir Thomas Herbert, he was rather more interested in their flavour than in their behaviour:

The land is also rocky and sandy, without any fresh water, trees, or shrubs, or any land animal, except fowls, as boobies, but above all, penguins, a sort of sea-fowl of the bigness of a duck, and having just such feet, but the bill is pointed; their wings are no more than stumps, which serve them instead of fins in the water; and they are covered rather with down than with feathers; As they feed on fish so their flesh is but of an indifferent taste, but their eggs are very good. The penguins are to be seen all over the South sea, on the coast of Newfoundland, and on the Cape of Good Hope.

A Historical Account of all the Voyages Round the World performed by English Navigators (1773) provides an account of a penguin they found in the Falkland Islands and attempted to bring back to Europe:

Three kinds of penguins breed on the island, one of these is a remarkably grand and elegant bird, the belly of which is clear white, the back a kind of blue, and it has a ruff round its neck near the head, of a bright yellow, which descending towards the belly separates the white feathers from the blue ones; these birds do not live together in numbers, but seek the most quiet and retired places of abode. One of them being caught, with an intention of being brought to France, soon grew so tame, that it followed the person who fed it; its food was bread, fish and flesh; but there was something more wanting its sustenance, for it gradually lost its fatness till it died.

It is interesting to note how similar all the descriptions of the penguins are, specifically the repeated image of the penguin's wing as a sleeve. It is possible that this repetition arises because each writer is referencing the descriptions that went before them. Equally, it could be that this is just an accurate way to describe the appearance of a penguin's wing.

Zebra

The following description of wild African zebras was included in Samuel Purchas's *Purchas his Pilgrimage* (1613):

The Zebra of all Creatures for beautie and comeliness is admirably pleasing: resembling a Horse of exquisite composition, but not all so swift, all over-laid with partie-coloured Laces and gards from Head to Taile.

This next description is from *The Strange Adventures of Andrew Battell of Leigh, in Angola and the Adjoining Regions* as featured in *Purchas his Pilgrimage* (1613). Andrew Battell (1565–1614) was an English privateer kidnapped by the Portuguese in 1590 and taken into the interior of Africa to Angola and the Congo. Battell returned to Leigh in Essex in 1610 and told his tale to Samuel Purchas, who included the narrative in his famous tome. Battell's story is said to be the first account of travels to this interior part of Africa. Thus his account of a wild zebra is likely to be one of the first European descriptions recorded:

Here is also the zevera or zebra, which is like a horse, but that his mane, his tail, his strakes and divers colours down his sides and legs do make a difference. These zeveras are all wild[4] and live in great herds, and will suffer a man to come within shot of them, and let them shoot three or four times at them before they will run away.

Kangaroo

Captain William Dampier was the first Englishman to set foot in Australia in 1688 after his trading ship, the *Cygnet*, landed on the northwest coast. Dampier became the first person to note Australia's large hopping animals.

Australia was formally colonised in 1788 when the English set up camp in Sydney Cove. Early colonists marvelled at the wildlife they encountered in this strange new continent.[5] In *An Historical Narrative of the Discovery of New Holland and New South Wales* (1786) John Fielding pulled together all of the existing accounts from early explorers of Australia, including Captain James Cook (1728–1779), Abel Tasman and Captain Dampier, to capitalise on public interest in the new country after Lord Sydney announced in 1786 his intention

---

4 Zebras were thought to be untameable and this was something of a red flag to those industrious Victorians, who believed everything should have a purpose. Wealthy financier Lord Rothschild (1868–1937) was one of many to try and domesticate the zebra. Rothschild paid a notable horse trainer, Mr Hardy, to tame the beasts. After two years of hard work the zebras were sufficiently broken and Lord Rothschild was able to demonstrate his victory over animal kind by driving a carriage pulled by four zebras to Buckingham Palace. Take that nature!

5 When one thinks of Australian wildlife the two animals that instantly spring to mind are the kangaroo and the koala. And yet, due to the shyness of the koala and its habit of sleeping high in the treetops during the daytime, it was seemingly not observed by early colonists. Indeed it was not first described until 1803 and even then the samples and pictures sent back to England somehow failed to gain the attention they merited and the animal went largely unrecorded and unnamed. Koalas remained rarely noticed by travellers and it was not until 1821 that A. Waterhouse gave the animal its proper scientific name of *Phascolarctos cinereus* in his *Natural History of Mammals*.

to set up a penal colony there. Fielding quotes from Captain Cook's account of the local wildlife:

The quadrupeds observed in this country are but few; consisting of dogs; and an animal called by the natives kanguroo, which, when full grown is as big as a sheep; the head, neck and shoulders very small in proportion to the other parts of the body; the tail nearly as long as the body. Thick near the rump, and tapering towards the end; the fore legs of the one that was killed by Mr. Gore,[6] which was a young one, and much under its full growth, measured only eight inches, while the hinder ones were two-and-twenty inches long; it goes in an erect posture, and its motion is by successive leaps, or hops, of a great length; the fore legs are kept bent close to the breast, and seemed to be of use only in digging; the skin is covered with a short fur, of a dark mouse or grey colour, excepting the head and ears, which bear a slight resemblance to those of a hare.

John White (*c.* 1756–1832) in his *A Journal of a Voyage to Botany Bay, in New South Wales* (1788) provides an excellent and thorough description of the kangaroo:

What animals we have yet met with have been mostly of the Opossum kind. The Kangaroo, so very accurately delineated by Captain Cook, is certainly of that class, and the largest animal seen in the country. One has been brought into camp which weighed a hundred and forty-nine pounds. The conformation of this animal is peculiarly singular. Its hinder parts have a great muscular power, and are, perhaps, beyond all parallel, out of proportion, when compared with the fore parts. As it goes, it jumps on its two hind legs, from twenty to twenty-eight feet, and keeps the two fore ones close to the breast; these are small and short, and it seems to use them much like a squirrel. The tail of these animals is thick and long; they keep it extended, and it serves as a kind of counter-poise to the head, which they carry erect, when bounding at full speed.

---

6   Mr John Gore circumnavigated the globe four times and is famous for being the first European to kill a kangaroo.

The velocity of a Kangaroo as far outstrips that of a greyhound, as that animal exceeds in swiftness a common dog. It is a very timid, shy, and inoffensive creature, evidently of the granivorous kind. Upon our first discovering one of them, as it does not use its fore feet to assist in running, or rather, jumping, many were of opinion that the tail, which is immensely large and long, was made use of by them in the act of progression; but this is by no means the case. Had it been used in such a manner, the hair would probably have been worn away from the part which, of course, must be applied to the ground. The tail, from its size and weight, seems to serve it for a weapon both of defence and offence; for it does not appear that nature has provided it with any other. Its mouth and head, even when full grown, are too small for it to do much execution with the teeth; nor is the conformation of either at all calculated for the purpose. Indeed, its fore feet, which it uses, as a squirrel or monkey, to handle any thing with, and which assist it in lying down, are too small, and out of proportion, as are all the superior parts, to admits of its either possessing or exerting much strength.

The female has a pouch or pocket, like the Opossum, in which she carries her young. Some have been shot with a young one, not larger than a walnut, sticking to a teat in this pocket. Others, with young ones not bigger than a rat: one of which, most perfectly formed, with every mark and distinguishing characteristic of the Kangaroo, I have sent to Mr. Wilson, of Gower Street, Bedford Square.

Every animal in this country partakes, in a great measure, of the nature of the Kangaroo. We have the Kangaroo Opossum, the Kangaroo Rat, &c. In fact every quadruped that we have seen, except the flying squirrel, and a spotted creature, nearly the size of a Martin, resembles the Kangaroo in the formation of the fore legs and feet, which bear no proportion to the length of the hind legs.

George Barrington (1755–1804) was a reformed thief and later Superintendent of the first convicts at Parramatta. He recorded his observations of kangaroos in *A Voyage to New South Wales* (1796):

In my walks I often fell in with the kangaroos, of which there are great numbers: they are about the size of a common deer, of a dark tan colour; its head, I think, resembles that of the mocock from the East Indies.

The hind legs are much longer than the fore, and with them they leap and spring forward with amazing rapidity, their fore feet seldom being seen to touch the ground; and, indeed, they are so very short, that it is not possible the animal can make great use of them in running: they have prodigious force in their tail, which is a principal part of their defence when attacked; they strike a blow with this weapon sufficient to break the leg of a man, or the back of a dog; it also assists them in their springs, which are truly surprising.

The native dog is much swifter than the kangaroo, and will attack them with great courage; the chase is seldom of long duration, the kangaroo being soon tired, and is generally overtaken in less than a quarter of an hour. When seized if he has no opportunity of using the tail to advantage, he turns upon the dog, and catching hold with the talons of his fore-paws, he flies at and strikes his adversary with those of his hind-feet, which are long, sharp, and of great strength; and, if the dog is not assisted, it frequently happens that he gets the better.

I have frequently seen the male kangaroos which, when sitting on their haunches, would measure at least from five feet eight to five feet ten inches in height; such an one would, I think, over-match any of the dogs; but I never ventured to try them singly. Having had several young native dogs given me, from time to time, I take great delight in kangaroo hunting; it is not only agreeable exercise, but produces a dish for the table, nearly as good as mutton; and, in the present dearth of livestock, is not an unacceptable present.

This much later description from 1894 in *Kangaroo and Kauri* by J. K. Arthur is far more fanciful than the earlier accounts:

The merit of the kangaroo's tail is sometimes acknowledged by making soup of it. The animal is said to have a grasshopper's hind legs, a rat's fore-paws, and a coat partly resembling the rabbit and partly the rat. In place of a cradle the mother-kangaroo is provided with a pouch in which she lays her babies. The young kangaroos would fare ill without this secure retreat and snug hiding-place on the least sign of danger.

Pelican

A New Voyage and Description of the Isthmus of America (1699) by Lionel Wafer describes the pelican and its sideline as a natty sailor's accessory:

The Pelican is a large Bird, with a great Beak, short legg'd like a Goose; and has a long Neck, which it holds upright like a Swan. The Feathers are of dark Grey; 'tis Web-footed. Under the Throat hangs a Bag or Pouch, which, when fill'd, is as large as both ones Fists. The Substance of it is a thin Membrane, of a fine, grey, ashy Colour. The Seaman kill them for the sake of these Bags, to make Tobacco-pouches of them; for when dry, they will hold a Pound of Tobacco; and by a Bullet hung in them, they are soon brought into Shape. The Pelican flies heavy and low; we find nothing but fish in his Maw, for that is his Food. His Pouch, as well as Stomach, has Fish found in it.

Elk & moose

The History of North and South America (1776) contains the following cautionary description of an Elk:

> *This animal is the size of a horse or mule, its flesh is very agreeable and nourishing, and its colour a mixture of light grey and dark red. They love the cold countries, and when the winter affords them no grass, they gnaw the barks of trees. It is dangerous to approach very near this animal, when he is hunted, as he sometimes springs furiously on his pursuers, and tramples them to pieces.*

The same book contains a description of a moose. One can only imagine the impression these huge animals must have had on those first Europeans to encounter them:

> *One of the most singular animals, of this and the neighbouring countries, is the moose deer, of which there are two sorts: the common light-grey moose, (resembling the ordinary deer) which herd sometimes*

thirty together; and the large black moose, whose body is about the size of a bull, his neck resembles that of a stag, and his flesh is extremely grateful. The horns when full grown, are about four or five feet from the tip, and have shoots, or branches to each horn, which generally spread about six feet. When this animal goes through a thicket, or under the boughs of a tree, he lays his horns back on his neck, to place them out of his way, and these prodigious horns are said to shed every year; but this is, perhaps, a vulgar error, and similar to that which some writers assert respecting the elephant, who is said to have a new tusk annually.

Male moose do in fact shed their antlers annually, after the mating season. It then takes a moose between three and five months to grow a new set of antlers.

Cuttlefish

Some early descriptions reveal the amazement experienced by adventurers when they came across a beast so foreign to anything they had ever seen before. John Fryer (*c.* 1650–1733) in his *A New Account of East India and Persia being Nine Years Travels 1672–1681* nicely encapsulates that wonder in his description of a cuttlefish (which, now you come to mention it, is a strange looking beast):

The Crafty Cuttle-Fish its dark Politicks … That it emits a black and cloudy Liquor to disturb the cunning Angler; the Truth whereof I could

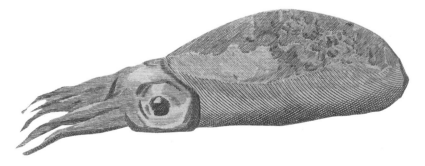

never observe; only what was more certainly miraculous, its monstrous
Figure: The Body was of a duskish Colour, all one Lump with the Head,
without scales; it was endowed with large Eyes, and had long shreds like
Gorgon's Hair, hung in the manner of Snakes, bestuck with snail-like
Shells reaching over the body; under these appeared a Parrot's Beak, two
Slits between the Neck are made instead of Gills for Respiration ... the
Inky Matter is bred in the Stomach.

Rattlesnake

Sometimes the explorers' ideas about
the natural world are really quite
quaint to modern eyes. Here in the
1776 book *The History of North and
South America*, the author paints the
picture of a more ordered and rule-
bound nature:

*The rattle-snake seems to be the only reptile in this country worthy of
our notice, some of which are as thick as a man's leg, and five or six feet in
length. The tail, which is the most remarkable part of this animal, is scaly
like a coat of mail, and on which, it is said, there grows every year one
ring, or row of scales. By this its age is readily discovered.[7] In moving, it
makes a rattling noise, and from hence it derives its name. The bite of this
serpent is mortal, if a remedy is not instantly applied; but Providence has
been pleased to direct it, that wherever this serpent lurks, a plant grows,
which affords an infallible cure to the wounded person. The rattle-snake
seldom bites passengers, unless it is provoked, and never darts itself at
any person without first rattling his tail three times.*

---

7   In fact a rattle is added each time the snake sheds its skin, which when young
and growing fast can be many times a year and when older can be less than once a
year; thus the number of rattles does not relate to the age of the snake but can reveal
how many times it has shed its skin.

Chameleon

The Roman author Pliny (AD 23–79) described the chameleon in his *Naturalis Historia*, thereby sparking a fascination with the colour-changing reptile. It seems likely that Pliny never actually saw a chameleon given that the creature he describes is as big as a crocodile. However, his description seemed to capture the public's imagination.

In the seventeenth century King Louis XIV had a chameleon amongst his menagerie at Versailles and when it died some prominent naturalists of the day were allowed to dissect it at the Royal Academy. One of these naturalists, Claude Perrault, wrote in *Memoires de l'Academie Royale de Science depuis 1666 jusqu'a 1699*: 'There is hardly an animal more famous than the chameleon. Its changing colour and peculiar manner of eating have given to students of nature in past centuries much to admire and study.'

Thus it is interesting to note that this 1670 account by Nicolas Villault in *A Relation of the Coasts of Africk called Guinee* of a chameleon attempts to refute the commonly held view that chameleons could change their colour:

They have Dragons also, and a sort of great Lizards, which are good to eat; they have Serpents of unmeasurable bigness, as also Crocodils, and Cameleons; these last are about the bigness of our green Lizards in France, and do not change their colour, as is imagined, but having their skins firm and scaly like glass, they represent variety of colours according to the different reflections upon them, which is the ground of that errour.

A later account by John Willock in *The Voyages and Adventures of John Willock, Mariner* (1798) contains an excellent and accurate[8] description of a chameleon:

One of our men laid hold of a camelion, the first I had ever seen. This little animal is about seven inches long from the top of the nose to the end of the tail. Its head resembles that of a frog, and it has four legs, very short, with feet which likewise resemble a frog's. One remarkable property of this animal, is its changing its colour. It is generally found in a woody country, most commonly on a bush or tree, and its colour is sure to resemble that fruit produced by the tree where you take it. It is said to live upon air. Certain it is, it is never seen to eat any thing, and it is probable the flies and other insects that inhabit the air, answer all its purposes.

Walrus

Journal of a Voyage undertaken by order of His Present Majesty for making discoveries towards the North Pole (1788) by Commodore Phipps (1744–1792) contains this wonderful description of a walrus (although it seems at this time they were not known by this name):

The sea-horse is a creature peculiar to high latitudes, is therefore more rare. It is not easy to say how it came by its name; for there is no more likeness between a sea-horse and a land-horse, than there is between a whale and an elephant. The sea-horse is not unlike the seal in shape. He has a large round head, larger than that of a bull, but shaped more like that of a pug-dog without ears, than any other animal we are acquainted with. He tapers all the way down to the tail, like the fish we call a lump, and his size is equal to that of the largest sized ox. His tusks close over his under jaw, like those of a very old boar, and are in length from one foot to two or more, in proportion to the size and age of the animal that breeds them. His skin is thicker than that of a bull, and covered with short

---

8   If we ignore the bit about them surviving on air, by which he probably means that it eats only airborne insects.

mouse coloured hair, which is sleeker and thicker, just as he happens to be in or out of season when he is caught. His paws, before and behind, are like those of a mole, and serve him for oars when he swims, and for legs to crawl when he goes upon the ice, or on shore. He is a fierce animal, but being unwieldy when on land, or on the ice, is easily overcome.

These animals are always found in herds, sometimes of many hundreds together, and if one is attacked, the rest make a common cause, and stand by one another till the last gasp ... some of them have been known to make holes in the bottom of the boat with their tusks, in defence of their young. Their eyes are large, and they have holes in the upper part of the neck, out of which they eject the water in like manner as it is ejected by whales.

This later account from Professor Leslie, Professor Jameson and Hugh Murray in their 1844 book *Discovery and Adventure in the Polar Seas and Regions* showed that, as ever, we humans have found novel ways to utilise the wonders of nature:

All the shores and borders of the Arctic zone are crowded with huge amphibious races, which appear to form an intermediate link between whales and quadrupeds, – the mammalia of the sea and those of the land. Among these is to be distinguished the morse or walrus (trichecus rosmarus), which bears such a resemblance to our domestic quadrupeds, that sailors, according to their various impressions, have given it the title of sea-horse or sea-cow. It is a large, shapeless, unwieldy creature, 12 to 15 feet in length, and from 8 to 10 in circumference; the head small, the limbs short, of an intermediate character between fins and legs. As a defence against the extreme cold, these animals not only have skins an inch thick, covered with close hair, but enjoy like other cetacea a coating of oily fat, with which their bodies are completely enveloped. Thus cased, they lie stretched on the ice in the depth of winter, without suffering any inconvenience. The most remarkable feature of the walrus, however, consists in two teeth or tusks, which project in a curved line from the upper jaw, and are nearly two feet in length. They are of beautiful white bone, almost equal to ivory, and much used in the fabrication of artificial teeth.

Lion

Lions have been known in Europe since Roman times, having been exported to menageries or captured to perform at circuses. Lions were quickly adopted as a symbol of royalty, bravery and nobility – a theme that has proved enduring. Because of the widespread depictions of lions in European culture even ordinary people were familiar with a lion's appearance. Therefore it was the character of the lion that seemed to attract the explorers' descriptions.

In *Purchas his Pilgrimage* (1613) the following theory on the ferocity of lions was put forward:

> *The Lions in cold places more gentle, in hotter are more fierce, and will not flee the onset of two hundred horse-men armed.*

In *The True Travels, Adventures and Observations of Capitaine John Smith, in Europe, Asia, Africa, and America 1593–1629* (1630) the sad tale of a very loyal lion captured in Morocco is recounted:

> *Not farre from Mount Atlas, a great lionesse in the heat of the day, did use to bathe her selfe, and teach her young puppies to swimme in the river Cauzeff, of a good bredth; yet she would carrie them one after another over the river; which soome Moores perceiving watched their opportunitie, and when the river was betweene her and them, stole foure of her whelps, which she perceiving, with all the speed shee could passed the river, and comming neere them they let fall a whelp (and fled with the rest) which she tooke in her mouth, and so returned to the nest: a Male and a Female of those they gave Mr Archer, who kept them in the Kings Garden till the Male killed the Female, then he brought it up as a Puppy-dog lying upon his bed, till it grew so great as a Mastiffe, and no dog more tame or gentle to them hee knew: But being to returne to England, at Saffee he gave him to a Merchant of Marsellis, that presented him the French King, who sent him to King James, where it was kept in the Tower seven yeares. After one Mr John Bull, then servant to Mr Archer, with divers of his friends, went to see the Lyons, not knowing any*

thing at all of him; yet this rare beast smelled him before hee saw him, whining, groaning, and tumbling, with such an expression of acquaintance, that being informed by the Keeper how he came thither; Mr Bull prevailed, the Keeper opened the grate, and Bull went in: But no Dogge could fawne more on his Master, than the Lyon on him, licking his feet, hands and face, skipping and tumbling to and fro, to the wonder of all the beholders; being satisfied with his acquaintance, he made shift to get out of the grate. But when the Lyon saw his friend gone, no beast by bellowing, roaring, scratching, and howling could expresse more rage and sorrow, nor in foure days after would he either eat or drinke.

The author of *The Adventures of Mr T. S. an English Merchant Taken Prisoner by the Turks of Algiers* (1670) also saw lions in Morocco; he too is struck by the character of the lions he encounters, so much so that he rather anthropomorphises the beasts:

We saw several sorts of Lions; towards the Evening they did go out of their Dens, when the Jackals began to bark.
    The noblest sort of Lion is that which is called the Royal; it is the biggest and the strongest sort; it hath a Shape somewhat differing from the rest, and a Voice more stout: When any of the others do meet such an one, they seem to yield a respect unto him. He is more grave in his Motion, more fierce in his Encounter, undaunted in the greatest danger.

Once again another traveller, John Mocquet in his 1696 *Travels and Voyages into Africa, Asia and America, the East and West-Indies; Syria, Jerusalem and the Holy-Land* observes some lions in Morocco and perceives that nobility of character which had made lions such a potent royal symbol:

After this I went to see the Lions, which were shut up in a great ruinous House, open at the top, and to be mounted one pair of Stairs; and saw there many remarkable things, but one more particularly, which was concerning a Dog, who had formerly been cast to the Lions for their Food; for one of the Lions (and the oldest of all the others who feared

him) took this Dog that had been cast in under his Paws, as if he would have devoured him; but having a mind to play a little with him before, it happened that this Dog flattering the Lion, as knowing his Strength, began to scratch him gently with his Teeth upon a scab which the Lion had upon his Throat; at which, the Lion took such pleasure, that he not only suffered the Dog patiently so to do, but also defended him from the others: So that when I saw him, he had been then seven years with these Lions, as the Christian Slave told me who look'd after them; and told me also, that when they gave the Lions any thing to Eat, the Dog fed with them, and would sometimes snatch the Meat from their very Chops; And when the Lions would fight together for their Food, the Dog did all he could to part them, and when he saw he could not do it, by a Natural Instinct he began to howl after such a manner, that the Lions (who fear the cry of Dogs) presently would part themselves, and agree together.

Tiger & leopard

Tigers once roamed vast tracts of land from Asia through Russia and Turkey, and like the lion have been strongly represented in both myth and traditional folklore. Both the tiger (*Felis tigris*) and the leopard (*Felis pardus*[9]) were first officially described and named by the father of taxonomy Carl Linnaeus in *Systema Naturae* in 1758. Due to their beautiful pelts, big cats have long been much sought after by the hunter. Christopher Schweitzer in his *A Relation of a Voyage to and through the East Indies from the year 1675 to 1683* provides the following account of the 'tigers' of Ceylon (Sri Lanka), which are almost certainly leopards as tigers are not native to Sri Lanka:

Tygers are here also in abundance, and very pernicious to Man and Beast, and particularly to Stags and Deer. They are about the bigness of a large Ass, but something longer; they are spotted with yellowish and whitish spots, and in their Make exactly like a Cat. Their flesh is white, and many people Eat of it. Their skins serve to make Belts, Holsters &c. and are much used for covering of Trunks and Boxes. They have so much of the scent of Musk, that the Huntsmen, if they take the Wind right, will find them out by it, and so in their pursuit of other beasts, avoid them.

A New Account of East India and Persia being Nine Years Travels 1672-1681 (1698) by John Fryer has this description of an Indonesian tiger:[10]

Going in quest whereof, one of our Soldiers, a Youth, Killed a Tigre-Royal; it was brought home by Thirty or Forty Combies; so they brought it to the House, where we saw 'twas Wounded in Three Places, one through the Head with Two Bullets, another through the Body slanting up to the Shoulders, a Third in the Leg; it was a Tigre of the Biggest and Noblest Kind, Five Feete in Length beside the Tail, Three and half in height, it was of light Yellow, streaked with black, like a Tabby Cat, the Ears short, with a few bristles about the Lips; the Visage Fierce and Maje-

---

9   Leopards have been known by the Latin *Panthera pardus* since 1912 when Reginald Innes Pocock proposed the new species name, somewhat settling the debate over the correct taxonomical grouping of the leopard.

10 Tigers were once found across the islands of Indonesia but the Javan and Bali tiger are both now extinct, leaving only the critically endangered Sumatran tiger.

stick, the Teeth gnashing, Two of which she brake against the Stones for anguish, the Shoulders and Fore-legs thick and well-set, the Paw as Large as the biggest Fist stretched out, the Claws thick and strong.

Captain J. Forsyth (1838–1871) in *The Highlands of Central India* (1871) provides a very reassuring snapshot of tigers in India:

At the outset of one's experience in forest life it is impossible to avoid the belief that the tiger of story is about to show himself at every step one takes in the thick jungle; and it is not till every effort to meet with him has been used in vain that one realises how very little danger from tigers attends a mere rambler in the jungles. During ten years of pretty constant roaming about on foot in the most tigerish localities of the Central Provinces, I have only once come across a tiger when I was not out shooting, and only twice more when I was actually searching for tigers to shoot. In truth, excepting in the very haunts of a known man-eater, there is no danger whatever in traversing any part of the jungles of this, or I believe any other, part of India.

A 'counterfeit' lamb

Some people's experiences of life in exotic countries made them quite keen to see marvellous and magical beasts at every turn. This wonderful account of a mysterious animal by an Englishman who spent five years in captivity in the Ottoman Empire is relayed in his book *The Adventures of Mr T. S. an English Merchant Taken Prisoner by the Turks of Algiers* (1670):

> I had almost forgot one of a strange Nature; it appear'd unto us as a White Lamb, something differing in shape, as we were marching through a Valley; but when it perceived us to approach in such Numbers, it fled before us; our Captain thought it had been some straggling Lamb belonging to some Mountainous People, and because we were not well provided with good Victuals, he sent some of us to overtake it before it got into the neighbouring thickets of a rising Hill: I had Order to pursue it, and accompany the Hunters. As we came within a hundred Paces of it, it made more haste than ordinary, and began to shift for itself amongst the Trees; but as it could not well escape from us, because it was already weary, and very fat, we overtook it at the entry of the Bushes; but perceiving us so near, it ran under one, and that we might not find it, it changed in an instant its white colour into the same with the Bush, which unexpected alteration gave us a great deal of trouble. We had never found it again, had not one of the Company discharged a Musket; at the Noise it rose up in a fright, and began to run for its Life; we little thought it to be the same, nevertheless some of us did venture after it, and some remained in the place, seeking the white Beast: The Pursuers shot off one of its Legs, and then cried to us to forbear seeking, and that the counterfeit Lamb was caught. We went to be Eye witnesses of the Wonder; it was the same shap'd Beast, but the colour was no more White as before, the Milky Colour was changed into a Blackish Gray: Its Coat was a fine Wool, the Head was like a Wolf, not altogether so long, it had very sharp Teeth, and a fierce Look, the Hinder-parts were like a Sheep: It is one of the strangest Creatures I ever saw. I wondered how it could alter its White Wool into a Colour so different: I imagined this to be the Beast

mentioned by the Learned, that takes the Colour of the place where it lays; a good Emblem of an Hypocrite.

Mr T. S. seems convinced this was a queer beast that could change colour, rather than considering the idea that one type of animal went into the bush and quite another came out.

Flamingo

Captain William Dampier in *A New Voyage Round the World* (1699) wrote about the now iconic flamingos he saw in Cape Verde:

I have also seen some wild fowl here, and especially the Flamingoes, a reddish fowl, of the shape of a heron, but much larger, living in ponds, or muddy places: We shot about fourteen of them, though they are very shy: Their nests they build with mud, in the shallow places in ponds or standing waters; these they raise up like hillocks, tapering to the top, two feet above the surface of the water, where they leave a hole to lay their eggs in, which when they do, or are hatching them, they stand with their long legs in the water close to the hillocks, and so cover the hollowness only with their rumps; for if they should sit on them, the weight of their bodies would break them. The young ones cannot fly, nor do they come to their true colour or shape till they are ten or eleven months old, but run very fast: They have large tongues and near the root of them, a piece of fat, which is accounted a great dainty.

Elephant

Although elephants had been known in Europe since Roman times, their impressive size and form meant that they made a huge impression on anyone seeing one in the wild for the first time. In *Richard Eden's Account of John Lok's Voyage to Mina 1554–5*, the author first comes across an elephant's head kept as a curiosity in the house of Lord Mayor of London Sir Andrew Judde (d.1558):

> *At this last voyage, was brought from Guinea the head of an elephant of such huge bignesse that onely the bones or cranew thereof, beside the nether jaw & great tusks, weighed about two hundred weight, and was as much as I could well lift from the ground; insomuch that, considering also herewith the weight of two such great teeth, the nether jaw with the lesse teeth, the tongue, the great hanging eares, the bigge & long snout and troonke, with all the flesh, braines, and skinne, with all other parts belonging to the whole head, in my judgement it could weigh litle lesse than five hundred weight. This head divers have seene in the house of the*

worthy marchant, Sir Andrew Judde, where also I saw it, and beheld it,
not only with my bodily eyes, but much more with the eyes of my mind
and spirit, considering by the worke the cunning and wisedome of the
workemaister; without which consideration, the sight of such strange
and wonderfull things may rather seeme curiosities then profitable
contemplations.

The author himself then travelled to Africa and had the pleasure
of seeing some live elephants:

The elephant (which some call an oliphant) is the biggest of all foure
footed beasts, his forelegs are longer then his hinder, he hath ancles in the
lower part of his hinder legges, and five toes on his feete undivided; his
snout or tronke is so long and in such forme that it is to him in the stead
of a hand, for he neither eateth nor drinketh but by bringing his tronke
to his mouth, therewith he helpeth up his master or keeper, therewith
he overthroweth trees. Beside his two great tusks, he hath on every side
of his mouth foure teeth, wherewith he eateth and grindeth his meate;
either of these teeth are almost a span in length, as they grow along the
jaw, and are about two inches in height and almost as much in thick-
nesse. The tuskes of the male are greater then of the female. His tongue
is very little and so farre in his mouth it cannot be seene. Of all beastes
they are most gentle and tractable.

Edward Terry (1590–1660) made these observations of elephants
he saw in India, in his book *A Voyage to East-India: wherein some*
things are taken notice of ... (1655):

But for the Elephants ... they are very huge vast overgrown Creatures,
some of them which I have seen, I conceive at the least twelve foot
high, but there are amongst them (as they say) fourteen or fifteen foot
in height. The colour of them all is black; their skins thick and smooth
without hair; They have full eyes, but not proportionable to their great
bodys, they have ears like our Oxen, but not exceeding large, and those
ears edged (as it were) about with a shirt hair-fringe; and at the end of

their tayls (which are slender and not very long) there growes some hair
likewise and little on their eyelids; but no where els about their bodyes.

The feet of the Elephants look like the trunks of small trees cut square
off from their roots, round about which there are thick, and short, and
broad claws growing.

Some that write of them have abused the world with this tradition
that they have no joints in their legs, and therefore stand when they sleep
against trees to hold them up, which is all very false, for they ly down
and arise again at their pleasure as other beasts do.

Unfortunately not all travellers were there to admire the elephant;
some were there to hunt it. George Barrington in his *A Voyage to New
South Wales* (1796) recounted his experience of an elephant hunt in
Africa:

One of the Hottentots [native Khoikhoi people; the term is now consid-
ered derogatory] ascended a tree; after looking round him, he clapped
his finger on his mouth as a token for us to be silent, then by opening and
closing his hand several times (a signal before agreed upon) gave us to
understand how many elephants he had discovered...

In a few minutes I was very near one of those enormous animals,
which I did not immediately perceive, not that fear had fascinated my
sight, but that I could scarce believe that the prodigious immoveable
mass beneath me was the animal we had so much wished to encounter.
It should be observed we were on a hillock which raised us above the back
of the animal: I still kept looking farther on, and rather took what was so
near me for a fragment of rock than a living creature. The Hottentot now
cried out, "See, see there! There he is," with a tone of the utmost impa-
tience. At length a flight of motion caught my eye, and immediately after
the head and tusks, which the enormous body had in part concealed,
were turned towards me: Monsieur, who was close behind me, without
losing time, let fly at him; I immediately followed his example, and both
shots took place in his head; he staggered and fell: the noise frightened
the rest, and they, to the number of thirty, scampered off as fast as their
unwieldy corporations would permit them.

In *A Relation of a Voyage to and through the East Indies from the year 1675 to 1683* Christopher Schweitzer describes the elephants of Ceylon (Sri Lanka):

Among the Wild ones, I will speak first of the Elephants. They are finer and more Docile than in other Countries. Therefore they catch a great many of 'em, which they make Tame, and fit for War, and send them to the Kingdoms of Persia, Surrat, the Great Mogul, and several other places; and the Dutch themselves make use of them in the Field.

I have been very curious in Searching into the Nature, Disposition, and Qualities of these Elephants; and for that purpose conversed much with those that Catch them, when they are young, and have myself help'd to catch 'em. I have found in them all a great deal of Cunning, and a good Memory, in which they seem to be almost Rational Creatures. They never forget a Master's kind usage; but that of a rough and cruel one, they on the other side, never leave unrevenged.

When they are Catch'd and Tame'd, they never Couple together. They carry their young ones seven years,[11] and this has been manifest by the Wild She-Elephants that have been taken, and kept in the Stables which they have for 'em at Gala, and have brought forth their young at seven years end after they were catcht.

Tho' they have no hair, except on the Tail and Ears, yet they swim very well. They'll live above 200 years, as has been seen in some whose Age has been designedly mark'd. They go together in the woods some 8, 10 or 20 in a Company. They have a sort of King, or Master-Elephant, which they follow; the young ones go in the middle.

The flesh of Elephants is not fit to eat, and their Hides are made no use of, by reason of their wanting Men to dress and prepare them. They are extream thick. The flesh is Spungy, and Rotts in two days or three days. The Hair that grows upon the Tail they hold very good against the Cramp, and as an approved Remedy they wear it made up in Rings on their Fingers.

---

11 Elephants in fact are pregnant for twenty-two months.

There seemed to have been a prevailing myth that the elephant could not kneel down, as a number of explorers mention this fact (generally to disprove it). *The True Travels, Adventures and Observations of Capitaine John Smith, in Europe, Asia, Africa, and America 1593–1629* (1630) contains this description of elephants from the Congo:

Elephants are bred over all those Provinces, and of wonderfull great-ness; though some report they cannot kneele, nor lye downe, they can doe both, and have their joynts as other creatures for use: with their fore-feet they will leape upon trees to pull downe the boughs, and are of that strength, they will shake a great Cocar tree for the nuts, and pull downe a good tree with their tuskes, to get the leaves to eat, as well as sedge and long grass, Cocar nuts and berries &c. which with their trunke they put in their mouth, and chew it with their smaller teeth.

Pedro Fernandez de Quiros (1565–1615) came across working elephants in the Philippines and they made a strong impression upon him. In his book *The Voyages of Pedro Fernandez de Quiros 1595 to 1606* De Quiros recounts some charming anecdotes about these majestic beasts, which reveal the intelligence and character he believed the elephants displayed:

It was a special sight to behold three elephants which were brought into the square, of which the largest, named Don Fernando, had been sent as a present from the King of Cambodia to the late Governor when he asked for help. On each one there was an Indian driver, dexterous in the method of governing the elephant, both by words and by the use of an iron hooked instrument. Placed in front with his goad, the driver made him run, march, go down on his knees, raise himself, and other things well worth seeing. The hook serves the same use as a bridle for a horse.

A few days afterwards (according to what was said), when this elephant was drinking at the river, there came to him a great and well-fed crocodile, which had taken many natives in that river. He seized the elephant by the trunk, and when the elephant felt it, he raised up the crocodile just as easily as a fishing rod raises a light fish, and let him fall on the ground without more ado. A crocodile, such as this one, weighs as much as a fat bullock.

They say also that this elephant had a boil on his gum, of which the native driver cured him, but the pain made him throw about his trunk so as to hurt his driver. When the elephant was about to be healed, the driver said to him: "I am very angry, Don Fernando, for in return for the good I did you, you tried to kill me. What do you think the King, my Lord and yours, who sent you here, and gave me for your companion to look after you, if he knew of it, would say? See how you can no longer eat, and are getting thin, and you will soon die without any fault of mine. Open your mouth, if you please, and presently I will cure you like a friend, forgetting the harm you did me." The elephant, having taken two turns with his trunk round a shelf that was there, opened his mouth, and was operated upon without moving, his groans showing what pain he endured. And so he was cured.

Of another elephant they told me that to avenge himself on a native who had charge of him, he crushed him when he passed through a doorway, and killed him. The man's wife said to the elephant: "Don Pedro, you have killed my husband. Who is now going to maintain me?" On which the elephant went to the market place, and took a basket of rice which it gave to her, and when it saw that she had eaten it all, it fetched another, and then another. Things are said of these animals which seem incredible, and the wonderful thing is that they understand everything, in whatever language is spoken, as I have myself seen. An elephant was surrounded by Spanish soldiers, and one told him, without making any sign, to take a plantain out of his pocket and eat it. The elephant promptly put his trunk into the pocket, and when he found that no plantain was there, he took up a little earth in his trunk, and threw it in the face of the soldier who had deceived him.

Elephants were not only used as transport. In *The Travels of Peter Mundy in Europe and Asia 1608–1667* (1667) he comes across fighting elephants in India:

In India are used many other fighting of beasts, as of Eliphants, wild Buffaloes etts. The fighting of Eliphants is seldome seene but where the King is, and there often used, sometymes twice a weeke, viszt. Tuesdaies and Sattardaies in the afternoone att Agra. The manner thus, partly as my selfe sawe, and partly by report. First the Elephants appoynted for the day, which are usually one Couple, other Tymes there may be two and some tymes three Couple. The King cometh to the Jarooca or windowe, that looketh into the River, upon whose stand, right before the said Windowe, being the place appoynted, they are brought; with each guide sitting on his Neck. Att the word given they are lett goe, and so runninge one against the other with their Truncks aloft they meete head to head. There they with their Teeth lye Thrustinge and forceinge with all their strength, whoe are againe parted by their Keepers. But some-tymes they will not be ruled by words. Then doe they apply fireworks on long Bamboes or staves betwene them, whose cracks and noyse, fire and smoake doe sever them (for they stand much in feare of it), soe lett them joyne againe; this as often as they please. Sometymes one getts the victorie by over bearing the other in strength till hee make him give way, which hee followes; and if the other bee not too light for him, overtakes and overthrowes him sometymes, then lyes over him, foyninge [thrust-ing] att him with his teeth, tramplinge and over-lyeing him, for they can neither kick, bite nor Scratch. Theis fighting Eliphants are of the fairest bignesse and strongest, whose teeth are sawen off in the middle and then bound about with iron or Brasse for there more strength; for if they were left whole, they endaunger the breakeing att every encounter ... There Keepers or Guides are many tymes strucken of in the fight, but quickly gett up againe; but sometymes they are killed outright. Other tymes they are left to run after men on horseback, whoe are too nimble for him; for the Eliphant cannot gallop, only shoveling away hee may run somewhat faster then a man.

Dolphin

In the fantastically titled *A Voyage to East-India: wherein some things are taken notice of...* (1655) Edward Terry writes about the dolphins he watched from his ship. What starts as a lovely whimsical musing on these majestic creatures quickly goes the way of many of these accounts by very hungry sailors:

The Dolphin is a fish called for his swiftnesse the Arrow of the Sea, differing in this one particular from all other fishes I ever observed, in that he hath many little teeth upon the top of his tongue; Hee is very pleasing to the eye, smell and taste, of a changeable colour, finn'd like a Roach, covered with many small scales, having a fresh delightsome sent above other fishes, and in taste as good as any; these Dolphins are wont often to follow our ships, not so much I think for the love they bear unto man (as some write) as to feed themselves with what they find cast overboard, whence it comes to pass that many times they feed us, for when they swim close to our ships wee often strike them with a broad instrument, full of barbs, called an Harping-iron fastened to a roap, by which we hale them in; This Dolphin may be a fit Embleme of an ill race of people, who under sweet countenances, carry sharp tongues.

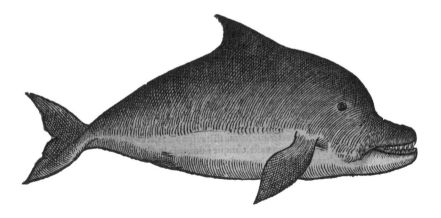

Shark

Picture the scene: another baking hot day aboard ship, the crystal waters of a tropical paradise lapping invitingly against the bow. The sailors, untainted by the horrors of *Jaws*, dive into the welcoming cool of the ocean, little suspecting what lies beneath ...

Judging by this collection of accounts, there was a fair amount of naivety in relation to the hazard presented by sharks. This was unsurprising perhaps for Europeans for whom back home sewage probably presented the greatest danger in the water. *A Short Journey in the West Indies in which are interspersed Curious Anecdotes and Characters* (1790) contains this rather horrifying tale:

> *Never having been in the West Indies, the stories concerning sharks had made no impression on my memory, and when he first cried out A fish! The warning was not accompanied, in my imagination, with the idea of danger.*
>
> *Some of the men, who were swimming, begged he would not frighten them with false alarms: however, he had scarcely spoken before we were all convinced that the alarm was but too just. From the gangway, where I was sitting with my legs over, I perceived through the clear water a fish, which as it approached (and that it did with wonderful rapidity) seemed to grow larger and larger, till it became, what it really was, a horrible monster.*
>
> *Figure to yourself a number of men, naked, whose forms are completely visible, in the height of sport and enjoyment, suddenly turning their eyes upon a prodigious animal, to which one of them must inevitably and immediately fall a prey! Then paint them, making instantly one and all for the boat, with that imperfect activity which fear and foreign element occasion; and more so when compared with the speed of their voracious pursuer.*
>
> *With the swiftness of an arrow he is in the midst of them. –The poor Armourer – I saw him as clearly as I now do the pen in my hand – the enormous creature made first at him; but, with the most surprising presence of mind, at the moment the shark turned, to make his bite,*

he precipitated himself to the bottom. The monster's eyes being caught by other objects before him, he did not pursue the Armourer, but made instantly to the ship; where he came but too soon for a poor fellow, who had already one hand upon the boat, into which half a minute more would have seen him safe: – but his fate was otherwise determined ... The devoted lover, pale as the death that awaited him, with his left hand clinging to the boat, looked on his approaching fate without uttering a single sound. He and the shark were now directly beneath my feet, not two yards below. The mouth of this animal being placed under its head, forces it to turn on its side when it would seize any thing. When he made this turn, he opened such a mouth, that I thought he would have swallowed the man up; but, with his right hand he darted a blow forward, and the monster took off his arm close to the shoulder. I now hoped he would have gone, for a man in the boat had pierced him once or twice with the boat-hook; but, ravenous beyond conception, he made another turn, and seizing the unfortunate youth by the waist, he coloured the water a little with his blood, and went off with him with as much rapidity as he had come.

Another adventurer who soon discovered the danger posed by sharks was Dutchman Christopher Fryke, who recounted his unfortunate experience in *A Relation of Two Several Voyages made into the East Indies* (1700):

These sharks we as often call Men-Eaters in Dutch, because they are very greedy of men's flesh. They have a large Mouth, which they open very wide, and Teeth of great length, and exceeding sharp, which shut into one another; so that whatever they get between them, they bite clear through. They are about 20 or 24 Foot in length; and they keep about the Ships in hopes of Prey; but are much more frequent in the Indies, than in the Way; where they do abundance of Mischief among the Seamen when they go to swim, as we afterwards found, when we came in the Road near Batavia where one swimming at a distance from the Ship, a Shark came up to him, and drew him under the water, and we never could hear of him more, or so much as see any remnant of him; which made all the old Seamen wonder, who said, They never knew a Shark take any more of a Man, than a Leg, or, it may be, a good Part of the Thigh with it: But for this Man, we did not perceive so much as the Water bloody. Near Japara we had a Man, who had lost a Limb by this means, under our hands to cure; and he lived seven Days after it; but at the end of that time he died, being mightily tortured with a vehement Cramp. Another time, at the Isle of Onrust, about eight Leagues from Batavia [Jakarta, Java, Indonesia], our Ship being layed up to mend something of the side of it, the Carpenter going to do something to it, about a Knee deep under Water, had his Arm and Shoulder snap'd off. I took him and bound him up, but to no purpose; for in less than three Hours time, he was dead.

And so it continues. *The Travels of Peter Mundy in Europe and Asia 1608–1667* (1667) contains this observation:

Amonge the severall sorts of Fishes aforementioned, I will only decipher the Sharke. The Sharke is verie daringe ravenous fish, soe that by report hee often seiseth on men and boyes as they are swimminge in the Sea quite sheireing of [the flesh] where soever hee lays hold on, of about 6 or 7 foote longe, appearing most comonly in Calmes, accompanied with

small Pilate Fishes and little suckinge fishes sticking on his back with their bellies upwards.

Edward Terry in *A Voyage to East-India: wherein some things are taken notice of...* (1655) is rather more preoccupied by musing on the psyche of the shark:

The Shark hath not this name for nothing; for he will make a morsell of any thing he can catch, master and devour. These sharks are most ravenous fishes; for I have many times observed, that when they have been swimming about our Ships (as oftentimes they doe) and we have cast overboard an iron hook made strong for this purpose, fastned to a roap strong like it, bayted with a piece of beefe of five pounds weight, this bayt hath been presently taken by one of them, and if by chance the weight of fish, thus taken in hauling him up hath broken out the Hooks hold, not well fastned (as sometimes it did) so that he fell into the Sea, he would presently bite at an other bayte, and so bite till he was taken. Not much unlike many vile men, who think they may safely take any thing they can finger and get, and having been fastened in, and escaped out of many snares, will take no warning ... [and] will take them at last and hamper them to their unavoydable destruction.

Many of these shark grow to a very large greatness; they have a broad round head, in which are three rowes of teeth very strong and sharp, by which they are able to take off the leg of a man with one bite, as some have found by wofull experience while they have been carelessly swimming in these hot Seas, where these Sharks most use, and certainly were they as nimble as they are mischievous, would doe very much hurt.

But it was not all one-way traffic and our plucky explorers were not averse to beating the shark at its own game. Here Captain William Dampier in his *A New Voyage Round the World* (1699) reveals his experiences hunting the shark:

Of the sharks we caught a great many, which our men eat very favourably. Among these we caught one, that was eleven feet long. The space between its two eyes was twenty inches, and eighteen inches from one corner of the mouth to the other. Its maw was like a leather sack, very thick, and so tough, that a sharp knife could scarce cut it; in which we found the head and bones of an hippopotamus, the hairy lips of which were still found, and not putrefied; and the jaw was also firm, out of which we plucked a great many teeth, two of them eight inches long, and as big as a man's thumb, small at one end, and a little crooked; the rest not above half so long. The maw was full of jelly, which stunk extremely; however, I saved for a while the teeth, and the shark's jaw. The flesh of it was divided among my men, and they took care that no waste should be made of it, but thought it, as things stood, good entertainment.

Likewise Sinclair Thomson Duncan (1827–1927) in his *Voyage to Australia* (1884):

We had some sport on this day catching a shark, and as it was calm with a smooth sea, the fun was all the more enjoyable. We first saw him at the side of the ship, moving slowly through the water, evidently in search of something to eat, but he ultimately kept close by the quarter, sometimes near the stern. Immediately on it being known that a shark was near us, preparations were made by sailors to catch him, and for that purpose they secured a strong rope about the thickness of a man's finger, tied a large hook to the end of it, and then putting on a large piece of pork as a bait, which was thrown overboard, the shark gulped it eagerly, and was fast, and no mistake. I shall never forget the splash he made with his tail, and how desperately he struggled for freedom, while the sailors and others were singing out, "Hold on, my boys." But his efforts to get away were of no use, the hook had got a good hold in his throat. Two hardy sailors held on, another was ready with a rope having a running hitch on the end of it, which being flung near him, his tail got into the noose, and thus he was soon on the deck of the "Sussex," surrounded by a goodly number of spectators; and the scene was all the more interesting, when we took into consideration the fact that he was the first stranger which had visited us from the day we left England. He created no little amusement, especially to the children, as he struggled desperately to get into his own element, but in that he was never to be again alive, because no sooner were we satisfied in seeing his movements on the deck, than one of the sailors plunged a large knife into him, severing his head from the body, which led me to think that his struggles were over, but such was not the case as I noticed he still moved his tail. He was however soon cut up in pieces, and part of him eaten by some, who said he tasted well; but when I thought of him being a man-eater, I could not think of eating what others appeared to relish.

Polar bear

Commodore Phipps provides us with the, rather comedic, first recorded European sighting of a polar bear in his 1788 *Journal of a Voyage undertaken by order of His Present Majesty for making discoveries towards the North Pole*:

To the eastward lies Muffin's Island. Here they sounded, and found forty-five fathom water; rocky ground. Capt. Lutwich sent out the long boat, with orders to found along the shore, and to examine the soil. This island is about a mile long, very low, and looks at a distance like a black speck. Thought the soil is mostly sand and loose stones, and hardly so much as a green weed upon it, yet it is remarkable for the number of birds that resort to it in summer to lay their eggs, and breed their young; and these not of one kind only, but of many different sorts, as geese, ducks, burgomasters, ice-birds, malamucks, kirmews, rotgers, and almost every other species of bird peculiar to the climate; insomuch, that the eggs were so numerous and lay so thick upon the ground. That the men who landed found it difficult to walk without filling their shoes.

While the crew of the boat, ten in number, with their valiant officer at their head, were examining the island, after having found the shores, they observed two white bears making towards them, one upon the ice, the other in the water. Major Buz, for that was the officer's travelling title, like Falstaff was always the boldest man in company over a cup of sack, and minded killing a bear no more than killing a gnat; but seeing the bears approach very fast, especially that which came in the water, he ordered his men to fire while yet the enemy was at a distance, as he did not think prudent to hazard the lives of his little company in close fight. All of them pointed their muskets, and some of the party obeyed orders; but the greater part judging it safer to depend upon a reserved fire, when they had seemingly discharged their pieces, pretended to retreat. The Major, a full fathom in the belly, endeavoured to waddle after his companions; but being out of breath, and seeing the bear that came in the water had just reached the shore, thought of nothing now but falling the first sacrifice. His hair already stood on end; and looking behind him, he saw the bear at no great distance, with his nose in the air snuffling the scent. He had all the reason in the world to believe it was him that he scented, and he had scarce breath enough left to call to his men to halt. In this critical situation he unfortunately dropt his gun, and in stooping to recover it stumbled against a goose-nest, fell squash upon his belly into it, and had very nigh smothered the dam upon her eggs. The old saying is, Misfortunes seldom come alone. Before he could well rise, the enraged gander came flying to the assistance of his half-smothered consort and making a dart at the eye of the assailant, very narrowly missed his mark, but discharged his fury plump upon his nose. The danger now being pressing, and the battle serious, the bear near, the gander ready for a second attack, the men, who had not fled far, thought it time to return to the relief of their leader. Overjoyed to see them about him, but frightened at the bear just behind him, he had forgot the gander that was over his head, against which one of the men having levelled his piece fired, and he fell dead at the Major's feet. Animated now by the death of one enemy, he recovered his gun, and faced about to assist in the attack of the second. By this time the bear was scarce ten yards from him, and beginning to growl, the Major just in the instant was seized with a looseness, dropt his accoutrements, and fell back, that he might not be in the way of his party, to impede the engagement. In the hurry he was in, for a man of such valour we must not say the fright, he entangled his buttons, and not being able to hold any longer, he filled his breeches. The crew in an instant had brought down the bear, and now it was time for their leader to do something great. Having recovered his

54

arms, and seeing the poor beast grovelling on the ground, and growling out his last, like a ram in a pinfold, making a short race backwards in order to redouble his force, he came with nine long strides forwards, and with the strength and fierceness of an enraged bull, thrust his lance full four feet deep in the dying bear's belly.

On this ice, however, there were many bears, some of which came so near the ships as to be shot dead with small arms. These bears are very good eating, and where no better is to be purchased, the whalers account them as good as beef. They are many of them larger than the largest oxen, and weigh heavier. In many parts of their body they are musket proof, and unless they are hit on the open chest, or on the flank, a blow with a musket ball will hardly make them turn their backs. Some of the bears killed in these encounters weighed from seven to eight hundred weight; and it was thought, that the bear that routed the sailor's on Muffin's Island, could not weigh less than a thousand weight. He was, indeed, a very monster!

By the nineteenth century polar explorers had furnished the public with a few more facts about the great white bears. *A General History of Quadrupeds* (1800) contains this anecdote:

The ferocity of the Bear is as remarkable as its attachment to its young. A few years since, the crew of a boat belonging to a ship in the whale-fishery shot at a Bear at a short distance, and wounded it. The animal immediately set up the most dreadful yells, and ran along the ice towards the boat. Before it reached it, a second shot was fired, and hit it. This served to increase its fury. It presently swam to the boat; and in attempting to get on board, reached its fore foot upon the gunnel; but one of the crew having a hatchet, cut it off. The animal still, however, continued to swim after them till they arrived at the ship; and several shots were fired at it, which also took effect: But on reaching the ship, it immediately ascended the deck; and the crew having fled into the shrouds, it was pursuing them thither, when a shot from one of them laid it dead upon the deck.

Naturally what everyone really wanted to know was what a polar bear tasted like and if its body was any use to us humans. The book did not disappoint, adding:

Its flesh is white, and is said to taste like mutton. The fat is melted for train-oil; and that of the feet is used in medicine.

A rather colourful account of the polar bear is contained in *Discovery and Adventure in the Polar Seas and Regions* by Professor Leslie, Professor Jameson and Hugh Murray (1844):

In the caves of the rocks, or in the hollows of the ice, dwells the most formidable of Arctic quadrupeds, the Greenland or Polar bear. This fierce tyrant of the cliffs and snows of the north unites the strength of the lion with the untameable fierceness of the hyena. A long shaggy covering of white soft hair and a copious supply of fat enable him to defy the winter of this rigorous climate. Under the heat of Britain he suffers the most painful sensations; Pennant saw one, over whom it was necessary from time to time to pour large pailfuls of water. Another, kept for some years by Professor Jameson, evidently suffered severely from the heat of an Edinburgh summer.

The annals of the north are filled with accounts of the most perilous and fatal conflicts of the Polar bear. The first, and one of the most tragical, was sustained by Barentz and Heemskerke, in 1596, during their discovery of the north-east passage. Having anchored at an island near the strait of Waygatz, two of the sailors landed, and were walking on shore, when one of them felt himself closely hugged from behind. Thinking this a frolic of one of his companions, he called out in a corresponding tone, "who's there? Pray stand off." His comrade looked, and screamed out, "A bear! A bear!" then running to the ship, alarmed the crew with loud cries. The sailors ran to the spot armed with pikes and muskets. On their approach the bear very coolly quitted the mangled corpse, sprang upon another sailor, carried him off, and plunging his teeth into his body, began drinking his blood at long draughts.

Monkeys

A General History of Quadrupeds (1800) offers a delightful summation of the differing types of monkey:

On account of the numbers and different appearances of these animals, they have been divided into three classes, and described under the following denominations; viz. – APES, or such as have no tails; BABOONS, or such as have short tails; MONKIES or such as have long tails.

In the APE kind, we see the whole external machine strongly impressed with the human likeness, and capable of similar exertions: They walk upright, their posteriors are fleshy, their legs are furnished with calves, and their hands and feet are nearly like the human.

In the BABOON, we perceive a more distant resemblance of the human form: He generally goes upon all four, seldom upright, but when constrained to it in a state of servitude. – Some of them are as tall as a man – They have short tails, long faces, sunk eyes, are extremely disgusting, lascivious, and possessed of the most brutal fierceness.

The MONKEY kind are removed still farther, and are much less than the former. Their tails are generally longer than their bodies; and, although they sit upon their posteriors, they always move on all four. – They are a lively, active race of animals, full of frolic and grimace, greatly addicted to thieving, and extremely fond of imitating human actions, but always with a mischievous intention.

Christopher Fryke in *A Relation of Two Several Voyages made into the East Indies* (1700) recounts his experiences with monkeys in Indonesia:

On the other side of the Fort, is almost all Woods, which are cut down every other Year by the Soldiers. These Woods harbour vast numbers of Monkeys, which make there such a strange noise, that one would be amazed to hear it. We made it almost our daily diversion to go a Hunting after them, that a Man might have one of them for a Pipe of Tobacco. They are a very docile sort of Monkeys, and not in the least inferior to

those that are brought out of Africa and America for playing of Tricks.;
but they come but seldom over hither, being very tender, and not able to
bear the change of Climates, nor the hardship of so long a Voyage: For at
my return I took a couple of them with me, but as soon as ever we came
on this side of the Tropick, where we begun to feel a change of Air, they
were seized with the Bloody-Flux, fell lame, and died.

Fryke goes on to detail an ingenious method of capturing the beasts:

One way to catch them was, by taking of Coco-Nuts, which are very
plentiful there; and making a small hole in 'em, just big enough for 'em
to force their paws into; we hung them up all about the Trees where they
came. As soon as they espyed the hole, they wanting to get at the Kernel,
would strive hard but they would get their Paws in: And when they go
to take them out again, they have not the sense to squeeze their Claws
together to slip their Paws out, as they had to get them in: Besides that,
the surprize which the person causes, who watches them, makes them
less able to rid themselves of their Manacles; and as they went to run
down, they fall with the very weight of the Nut.

The playful character of monkeys frequently struck the explorers.
Lionel Wafer in *A New Voyage and Description of the Isthmus of*
America (1699) discovered this to his cost:

There are great Droves of Monkeys, some of them white, but most of them
black; some have Beards, others are beardless. They are of a middle Size,
yet extraordinary fat at the dry Season when the fruits are ripe; and
they are very good Meat, for we ate them very plentifully. The Indians
were shy of eating them for a while; but they soon were persuaded to it,
by seeing us feed on them so heartily. In the Rainy Season they have
often Worms in their Bowels. I have taken a handful of them out of one
Monkey we cut open; and some of them 7 or 8 Foot long. They are a
very waggish kind of Monkey, and plaid a thousand antick Tricks as we
march'd at any time through the Woods, skipping from Bough to Bough,
with the young ones hanging at the old ones Back, making Faces at us,

chattering, and, if they had opportunity, pissing down purposely on our Heads.

Dr John Francis Gemelli Careri in *A Voyage Round the World* (1700) was also fascinated by the character shown by the monkeys:

There are also in the Mountains, innumerable Monkeys, and Babboons so Monstrous big, that once at Samboangen, they say some of them defended themselves with Sticks, against a Pampango Souldier that assaulted them; so that the Souldier in a few days, dy'd with the Fright. The little Apes are diverting in the House. My Friend D. John del Poco had a white one; but so Old, that it held its Paw over its Eyes to see any thing, as a Man does, when he would observe something at a distance. He told me, he once had another of Borneo, which cry'd like an infant, and went upon two Feet, carrying a Mat under its Arm, to change its sleeping place. These Monkeys seem to be sharper in some respects then

Men, for when they can find no Fruit on the Mountains, they go down to
the Seaside to catch Crabs, Oysters and the like.

Many of the travellers attracted by the playful traits of the monkeys attempted to transport them back to Europe. John Mocquet in *Travels and Voyages into Africa, Asia and America, the East and West-Indies; Syria, Jerusalem and the Holy-Land* (1696) recounts his efforts to make a pet of a monkey:

I had also in exchange, of them, another sort of Creature, which is a kind
of an Ape or Marmot, but more Arch and Roguish, and with a very long
Tail. The Indians say that this Beast carries her young ones upon her
Back when she has cast them out of her Belly, and goes jumping from
Tree to Tree with them upon her Reins and when one of them is ready to
fall, she holds them up with her Tail.

This Animal makes such a noise about the Woods, that when they
are together tho' never so few, you would say there were a hundred Hogs
a killing.

That which I bought was Dead, and cost me a little Horn: It was a
Female having two Teats in the Stomach like a Woman. The Indians
had taken it with the Bow, and it had a stroke with an Arrow in the
Belly, and carried one of her young ones upon her Back; which they
brought us to sell for a Hatchet. This little one, being in our Ship, howled
after such a manner, that it made us all quite Deaf; it died afterwards,
for it would not Eat.

In *A True and Faithful Account of What was Observed in Ten Years Travells into the Principal Places of Europe, Asia, Africa and America* by R. F. Esq (1665) the author describes the tiny Brazilian Saguin monkey and its appeal as a pet:

Above all, the prettyest Animal Nature ever made is the Saguin, about
the bignesse of a little Squirrel, with long shag mains, and bushy tails, of
golden colour (most commonly) fac'd and handed like a Black-more, with
small fingers and smirking countenances; peeping or squeeking like a

Cricket when it craves, so as could it be but transported (as 'tis so tender and delicate, it commonly dies on change of air) all your Island Shocks, and Bollonian dogs would be banisht from Ladies Laps and Chambers, and these be their sole Minions and Favourites.

Orang-Utan

Orang-Utan means 'person of the forest' in Malay and is the name we now use for the tree-dwelling great apes of Southeast Asia. As accounts of great apes were collected from around the world it seems that at times the descriptions became confused or merged, as this entry from *A General History of Quadrupeds* (1800) attests. The description appears to encompass orang-utans and gorillas:

The Oran-Outang, or Wild Man of the Woods ... is the largest of all the Ape kind, and makes the nearest approach to the human figure.

The largest of its kind are said to be about six feet high, very active, strong and intrepid, capable of over-coming the strongest man: They are likewise exceedingly swift, and cannot be easily taken alive. – They live entirely on fruits and nuts, will sometimes attack and kill the negroes who wander in the woods, and drive away the Elephants that happen to approach too near the place of their residence. It is said that they some-times surprise the female negroes, and carry them off into the woods, where they compel them to stay with them.

When taken young, however, the Oran-Outang is capable of being tamed, and rendered extremely docile. – One of them, shewn in London some years ago, was taught to sit at table, make use of a spoon or fork in eating its victuals, and drink wine or other liquors out of a glass. It was extremely mild, affectionate, and good-natured; much attached to its keeper, and obedient to his commands. Its aspect was grave, and its disposition melancholy. It was young, and only two feet four inches high. Its body was covered with hair of a black colour, which was much thicker and closer on the back than on the fore part of the body; the hands and soles of the feet were naked, and of a dusky colour.

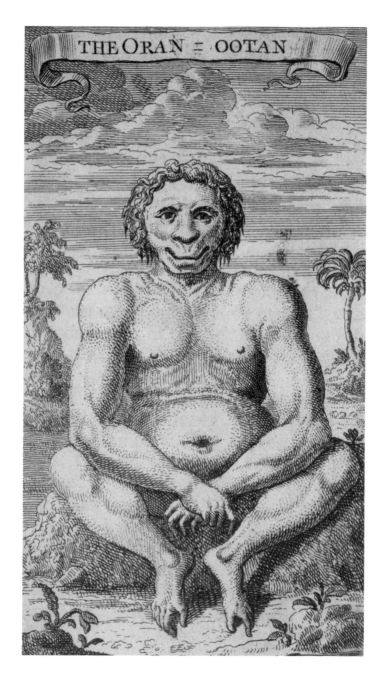

THE ORAN = OOTAN

Snake

A Voyage Round the World by Dr John Francis Gemelli Careri (1700) contains this marvellous description of a gigantic snake encountered in the Philippines (most likely the reticulated python, which can grow to up to 6 metres in length) and his somewhat bonkers theory on how the snake catches its prey:

There are snakes of prodigious Bigness. One sort of them call'd Ibitin, which are very long, hang themselves by the Tail down from the Body of a Tree, expecting Deer, wild Boars, or Men to pass by, to draw them to them with their Breath, and swallow them whole; and then winds it self round a Tree to digest them. Some Spaniards told me, The only Defence against them was to break the Air between the Man and the Serpent; and this seems rational, for by that means, those Magnetick or attracting Particles spread in that distance are dispers'd.

Monitor lizard or goanna

Captain William Dampier in his *A Voyage to New Holland, &c. in the year 1699* (1703), came across the Australian monitor lizard, known as a goanna, which made a lasting impression on him:

The Land-Animals that we saw here were only a sort of Raccoons, different from those of the West Indies, chiefly as to their legs, for these have very short fore Legs; but go jumping upon them as the others do, and like them are very good meat. And a sort of Guano, of the same shape and size with other guanos describ'd but differing from them in three remarkable Particulars: For these had a larger and uglier head, and had no tail: and at the rump, instead of the Tail there, they had a stump of a tail, which appear'd like another head; but not really such without mouth or eyes: Yet this created seem'd by this means to have Head at each end; and, which may be reckon'd a fourth difference, the Legs also seem'd all four of them to be fore-legs, being all alike in shape and length, and seeming by the Joints and Bending to be made as if they were to go indifferently either Head or Tail foremost. They were speckled black and yellow like Toads, and had Scales or Knobs on their backs like those of Crocodiles, plated on to the skin, or stuck into it, as part of the Skin. They are very slow in motion; and when a man comes nigh they will stand still and hiss, not endeavouring to get away. Their livers

are also spotted black and yellow: and the Body when opened hath a very unsavoury smell. I did never see such an ugly creature any where but here. The Guanos I have observ'd to be very good Meat: and I have often eaten of them with pleasure: But tho' I have eaten of Snakes, Crocodiles and Allegators, and many Creatures that look frightfully enough, and there are but few I should have been afraid to eat of if prest by Hunger, yet I think my stomach would scarce have serv'd to venture upon these N. Holland Guanos, both the looks and the smell of them being so offensive.

Duck-billed platypus

The duck-billed platypus is such an unlikely animal it is hardly surprising that when it was first noted by the Europeans it was dismissed as a hoax. The first specimens were shipped back to England for dissection in 1798 and one naturalist, George Shaw (1751–1813), noted in his work *Naturalists Miscellany* (1799):

Of all the Mammalia yet known it seems the most extraordinary in its conformation; exhibiting the perfect resemblance of the beak of a Duck engrafted on the head of a quadruped. So accurate in the similitude that, at first view, it naturally exhibits the idea of some deceptive preparation by artificial means.

The following account by Lieutenant-Colonel Collins (1756–1810) from *An Account of the English Colony in New South Wales Vol. II* (1802) is the first recorded description of a duck-billed platypus in the wild by a European:

Although the settlement had now been established within a month of ten years, yet little had been added to the stock of natural history, which had been acquired in the first year or two of its infancy. The Kangaroo, the Dog, the Opossum, the Flying Squirrel, the Kangaroo Rat, a spotted Rat, the common Rat, and the large Fox-bat (if entitled to a place in this society), made up the whole catalogue of animals that were known at

this time, with the exception which must now be made of an amphibious animal, of the mole species, one of which had been lately found on
the banks of a lake near Hawkesbury. In size it was considerably larger
than the land mole. The eyes were very small. The fore legs, which were
shorter than the hind, were observed, at the feet, to be provided with
four claws, and a membrane, or web, that spread considerably beyond
them, while the feet of the hind legs were furnished, not only with this
membrane or web, but with four long, sharp claws, that projected as
much beyond the web, as the web projected beyond the claws of the fore
feet. The tail of this animal was thick, short, and very fat; but the most
extraordinary circumstance observed in its structure was, its having,
instead of the mouth of an animal, the upper and lower mandibles of a
duck. By these it was enabled to supply itself with food, like that bird, in
muddy places, or on the banks of lakes, in which its webbed feet enabled
it to swim; while on shore its long and sharp claws were employed in
burrowing; nature thus providing for it in its double or amphibious
character. These little animals had been frequently noticed rising to the
surface of the water, and blowing like a turtle.

Such was the strange form and the shy nature of the duck-billed
platypus that it took many more years for the animal to be fully
observed and classified. It was not until 1864 that a specimen kept in

captivity at Woods Point, Victoria was observed laying two eggs – a circumstance which threw its classification as a mammal into doubt. When in 1884, W. H. Caldwell shot and killed a platypus, which had just laid an egg and on dissection was found to have another in its uterus, the unique status of the platypus was confirmed.

After much debate it was decided to create a new classification within the mammal grouping for both the duck-billed platypus and the echidna – monotreme. This classification covers these primitive animals which lay eggs (like reptiles and birds), but feed their young with milk, have three middle-ear bones and a single lower jaw bone (like mammals).

Dugong & manatee

It is claimed that the dugong or manatee was the inspiration for the mythical mermaid. Dr John Francis Gemelli Careri in his *A Voyage Round the World* (1700) was certainly confused by the sight of dugong in the Philippines:

> *The very fish of the Island have something very singular. One of these is the Duyon, by the Spaniards call Pece-Muger, that is Woman-Fish, because it has Breasts and Privities like a Woman, and there never was any Male seen. The bones of it have a notable Quality of stopping Bleeding, and curing a Cough. The flesh of it eats like Pork.*

Dugong and manatee are a related species and therefore are very similar, but the key visual difference is in their tail; the dugong has a fluked tail, like a whale's, whereas the manatee has a paddle-like tail. Dugongs are found in the coastal waters of Asia and the eastern coast of Africa, whereas manatees are found in West Africa, the Amazon and the Caribbean. *Voyages and Discoveries in South America* by Christopher D'Acugna (1597–1676) published in English in 1698 contains the following account of a manatee, observed in the Amazon River in Peru:

Fish is so common with 'em, that when any one offers it to 'em, they prover-
bially say, E'ne put it in your own Dish. There is so great a number of
'em in the River, that without any other Nets than their Hands, they can
take as many as they please. But the Pege Buey is as it were the King
of all the Fish that swim in the River Amazone, from its Source till it
discharges it self into the Sea. 'Tis not to be imagin'd what a delicious
Taste this Fish has, any one that eats it would think it to be most excel-
lent Flesh well season'd: This Fish is as big as a Heifer of a Year and a
half old, it has a Head and Ears just like those of a Heifer, and the body
of it is all cover'd with hair, like the Bristles of a white Hog; it swims with
two little Arms, and under its Belly it has Teats with which it suckles
its young Ones: The skin of it is very thick, and when 'tis dress'd into
leather it serves to make targets that are Proof against a Musquet Bullet.
This Fish feeds upon Grass on the Banks of the River, like an Ox, from
which it receives good Nourishment, and is of so pleasant a Taste, that a
Man is more strengthen'd and better satisfied in eating a small quantity
of it, than in eating twice as much Mutton.

Captain William Dampier in *A New Voyage Round the World* (1699)
noted these manatee in the Corn Islands of South America:

While we lay here, our Moskito men went in their Canoa, and struck us
some Manatee, or sea-cow. Besides this Blewfields River, I have seen of
the Manatee in the Bay of Campechy, on the Coasts of Boca del Drage,
and Boca del Toro, in the Rivers of Darien, and among the South Keys
or little Islands of Cuba. I have heard of there being found on the North
of Jamaica, a few, and in the rivers of Surinam in great multitudes,
which is a very low Land. I have seen them also at Mindanao one of
the Philipine Islands, and on the Coast of New Holland. This Creature
is about the bigness of a Horse, and 10 or 12 foot long. The mouth of it
is much like the mouth of a Cow, having great thick lips. The Eyes are
no bigger than a small Pea, the Ears are only two small holes on each
side of the Head. The biggest part of this Creature is at the Shoulders,
where it hath two large Fins, one on each side of its Belly. Under each
of these Fins the female hath a small Dug to suckle her young. From the

shoulders towards the Tail it retains its bigness for about a foot, then it groweth smaller and smaller to the very Tail, which is flat, and about 14 inches broad, and 20 inches long, and in the middle 5 inches thick, but about the edges of it about 2 inches thick. From the Head to the Tail it is round and smooth without any Fin but those two before mentioned.

Pangolin

The pangolin is a very curious creature, somewhere between an armadillo and an anteater. They are native to Asia and Sub-Saharan Africa. Pangolins are entirely covered by overlapping scales, and unfortunately it is the trade in these scales (which are used in traditional Chinese medicine) that have made the pangolin one of the world's most endangered species.

Sailmaker and adventurer John Struys (d.1694) observed a pangolin in Formosa (now known as Taiwan). He wrote of his experiences in *The Voyages and Travels of John Struys* (1684):

There is a certain Creature on this Island which the Hollanders call Den Duybel ban Tajovan; that is, The Devil of Formosa. Being about 2 foot long, and 5 inches broad upon the back, with scales all over the body, it has four feet with sharp claws, a sharp long head, and a tail thick at the rump and smaller towards the end, like a Crocodil. This little beast feeds only upon Pismires [ants], which he catches by laying his Tongue upon

upon a Hill where they come to feed upon a filmy matter, that runs out of his mouth, and that holds them so fast that they cannot get off again: When he thinks he has had enough, he draws in his tongue and devours them. It cannot do any harm unles to the Ants, which are its natural food, but if he see a man come towards him, either runs into the Earth, or rolls himself in, like a Hedghog: so that to call it a Devil seems a great impropriety.

Because of the pangolin's armoured exterior and long claws the poor insectivore was sometimes mistaken for a ferocious predator. *Francois Valentijn's Descriptions of Ceylon* (1724) by Francois Valentijn (1666–1727) contains this account of the frightful sounding Nigombo devil, which on analysis appears to be a benign Sri Lankan pangolin:

There are also the Nigombo devils here which are one yard tall, three yards long, four footed, with a very sharp and pointed mouth, sharp teeth and full of yellow shells which are round and like a harness on the body.

A Relation of a Voyage to and through the East Indies from the year 1675 to 1683 by Christopher Schweitzer contains a similar description:

There is a sort of Creature here, that is not very well known, because it is rare; it is called Bitsche Vergunie, and by the Dutch, The Devil of Negombo, which name they have given it, because of its Qualities, as I am going to tell you, and because they are most frequently about

Negombo. It is about a yard high, and three yards long. It hath a sharp
snout, and very sharp Teeth. The Body is as it were Harnass'd over with
thick round yellow shells. When it is pursued, it can winde itself up into
a Ball. At night it makes such a dismal frightful Noise, that it hath often
scar'd the Centinels from their Ports.

Sloth

Sloths are famed for their lack of speed; indeed these tree-dwelling
animals are so sedentary that algae grows on their fur, lending them
an extra bit of camouflage. Sloths spend most of their time sleeping in trees, waking at night to nibble some buds and leaves. Such
is their strong grip they have been known to remain hanging from
the tree even in death. Sloths are not able to walk on the forest floor,
instead they use their strong claws to drag themselves slowly back to
the safety of the trees.

Sloths were first noted by sixteenth-century Spanish explorers of
South America. *Summarie and Generall Historie of the Indies* (1555)
by Gonzalo Ferdinandez De Oviedo (1478–1557) contains the following account of a 'strange beast' which by his wonderfully evocative
description seems likely to have been a sloth:

There is another strange beast, which by a name of contrary effect, the
Spaniards call Cag-nuolo leggiero, that is The Light Dogge, whereas it is
one of the slowest beasts in the World, and so heavie and dull in moving,
that it can scarsly go fiftie paces in a whole day: these beasts are in the
firme land, and are very strange to behold for the disproportion that they
have to all other beasts: they are about two spans in length when they are
grown to full bigness, but when they are very young, they are somewhat
more grosse then long, they have four subtill feet, and in every one foure
claws like unto Birds, and joynd together, yet are neither their claws nor
their feet are able to susteine their bodies from the ground, by reason
whereof, and by the heaviness of their bodies, they draw their bellies
on the ground ... they have very round faces much like unto Owles, and

have a marke of their own haire after the manner of a Circle ... they have small eyes and round & nostrils like a Monkeyes ... their chiefe desire is to cleave and stick fast unto trees.

A Relation of a Voyage to and through the East Indies from the year 1675 to 1683 by Christopher Schweitzer includes this depiction of a beast which also appears to resemble a sloth:

The Lewer is another, called by the Dutch, Luiste Dier; i.e. Slow-Beast. These Beasts are made like an Ape, with Hands and Feet, look very ghastly, and as lean as a Skeleton, wonderful slow in their Eating, Drinking, and Going; tho' Dogs, or any Wild Beasts come towards 'em, they will not hasten their pace in the least; and when they come near 'em, they turn themselves to 'em, and with their glaring Eyes, fright away the fiercest Dog that can be. Their Eyes stand quite out of their Heads, and appear very terrible: When Men come after them they do the same: But it hath not the same Effect, for Men have a snare, which they clap on their hinder parts, and so catch them as they do Monkies. After they are catch'd, they are still slow as before, and would not go above a League in

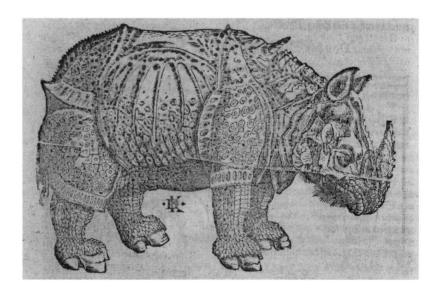

a day, if one left 'em to themselves. They are kept in Cities for a Rarity,
but they are too tender to transport into other Countries.[12]

Rhinoceros

Edward Terry provides the following description of a rhinoceros
that he encountered in India in his *A Voyage to East-India: wherein*
some things are taken notice of... (1655):

> *They have some Rhynocerots, but they are not common, which are very*
> *large square Beasts, bigger than the largest Oxen England affords; their*
> *skins, without hair, lye in great wrinkles upon their necks, breasts and*
> *backs, which doth not make them seem lovely unto the beholders. They*
> *have very strong but short Horns, growing upon very firm bones, that*
> *lye over their Nostrils, they grow upwards, towards the top of their head,*
> *every one of these Creatures being fortified with one of them, and that*
> *enough to make them so terrible, that they are shunn'd by other, though*
> *very large, Creatures. With these Horns (from which those Creatures*
> *have their Names) are made very excellent Cups, which (as is conceived)*
> *give some virtue unto the liquor put into them, if it stand any whit long*
> *in those Cups.*

Rhinoceros were considered as a possible source of the unicorn
myth by some (see Narwhal on p. 86)

Bat

Travellers used to the dainty bats of Europe were agog at the
Brobdingnagian bats encountered in the tropics. *The Narrative*

---

12 Two-toed sloths can survive for a long time in captivity and are housed
successfully in many zoos around the world. The three-toed sloth however is much
more difficult to transport and support in captivity outside the tropics due to their
limited and specialist diet and they are therefore still a very rare sight at zoos.

of Mendaña (1567) by Alvaro Mendaña (1542–1595), includes this anecdote:

In this island there are bats so large that, for fear of being accused of falsehood, I would not mention their size had they not been seen by everybody in the fleet. I measured one which we killed, and it measured more than three feet from the tip of one wing to the other; the head and body is like that of an ajo, with thick fur, and they have canine teeth.

In *A Relation of a Voyage to and through the East Indies from the year 1675 to 1683*, Christopher Schweitzer was equally impressed by the bats in Indonesia:

The 14th August came two Javans to Batavia, and brought Twelve Bats as big as Geese for a present to our General. They are reckon'd there a very delicate food; and I was told, they were brought to the General's Table as a Rarity, and fit for a great Entertainment. They fly out at Night as ours do, and haunt the Coco-Trees, and there suck the Suri that lies in the Coco-Nuts, so long, till they tumble down, and so are easily taken up with one's Hand; in the Day they keep in the Woods and hollow Trees.

The Travels of Peter Mundy in Europe and Asia 1608–1667 (1667) marvelled at the great size of the bats in Madagascar:

Also Batts, whose winges extand almost an English yard, their bodyes in forme and Coulour like Foxes, though noe bigger then a great Ratt. Theie hang all daye on trees by certaine hookes att the end of their winges, with their heads downewards, 4 or 500 together, and att night fly abroad.

Dr John Francis Gemelli Careri in *A Voyage Round the World* (1700) described the bats he witnessed in the Philippines:

This lake is small in Compass, but very deep, and in the middle of it they find no Bottom. The Water is Blackish, tho' it stands on a mountain not far from the great one, which may proceed from the Minerals under it. In it there is a sort of unsavoury bony Fishes. About it in the Day time there is an infinite number of large Bats, hanging on the Trees, one by another in Ropes. But towards Night they fly away in Swarms to the Woods a great distance off to get their Food, and sometimes they fly so thick together, that they darken the Air with their fleshy Wings, some of them six Spans long, which I was an Eye witness to whilst I staid at the aforesaid Bagnos, or the Baths. They know how to chuse in the thick Woods such Trees, whose Fruit ripens at certain Seasons, which they devour all the Night, making such a Noise that it is heard two Miles off. About break of Day they return to their Quarters. The Indians seeing the best Fruit God has provided for their sustenance, especially the Goyavas, and Pears, destroy'd by these scurvy Birds, kill all they can of them; and revenging themselves thus at once save their Fruit, and

provide themselves Meat, eating the Bats. They say their Flesh tastes like Rabbit, and indeed when they have slead them, and cut off their Heads, they are not at all unlike them.

Leaves which turn into insects

Some of the insects encountered by early adventurers were hard to fathom. In *A Voyage Round the World* (1700) Dr John Francis Gemelli Careri was puzzled to observe a tree with leaves that appeared to come alive:

The most wonderful thing of all, is that the Leaves of some Trees, when they come to a certain pitch of Ripeness, become living Creatures, with Wings, Feet, and Tail, and fly like any Bird, tho' they remain of the same colour as other Leaves. The Body is made of the hardest Fibers, in the middle, bigger or less according to the Leaf, that part joyning to the Tree, becomes the Head; the other end the Tail, the side-Fibres the Feet, the rest the Wings.

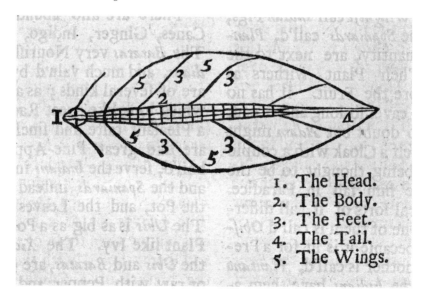

1. The Head.
2. The Body.
3. The Feet.
4. The Tail.
5. The Wings.

Careri is likely here describing an insect from the Phylliidae family – a creature that so closely resembles a leaf they even have brown tinged edges to their bodies, as if decomposing slightly, and move in such a way as to bring to mind the movement of a leaf blown by the wind.

Stick insect

A True and Faithful Account of What was Observed in Ten Years Travells into the Principal Places of Europe, Asia, Africa and America by R. F. Esq (1665) contains this wonderful description of a stick insect:

> *Another strange insect they have the Portuguez call Lobedio, or Praise God, as for some admirable thing, as indeed this is; It being a certain animated stick, like the end of some small twig, some fingers length, out of the joynts of which there grow out leggs by pairs, on which it crawls, like walking Tressles, nor can you perceive any other life it has, nor any other part of living Creature; as Eyes, Mouth, &c.*

Gorilla

When explorers first witnessed great apes such as gorillas they were not always certain whether the animal they saw was man or beast. *The Strange Adventures of Andrew Battell of Leigh, in Angola and the Adjoining Regions* as featured in *Purchas his Pilgrimage* (1613) includes this description of what is most likely a gorilla:

> *The woods are covered with baboons, monkeys, apes and parrots, that it will fear any man to travel in them alone. Here also are two kinds of monsters, which are common in these woods, and very dangerous.*
>
> *The greatest of these two monsters is called Pongo in their language, and the lesser is called Engeco. This Pongo is in all proportions like a man, but that he is more like a giant in stature than a man; for he is very*

tall, and hath a man's face, hollow-eyed, with long hair upon his brows. His face and ears are without hair, and his hands also. His body is full of hair, but not very thick, and it is of a dunnish colour. He differeth not from a man but in his legs, for they have no calf. He goeth always upon his legs, and carryeth his hands clasped upon the nape of his neck when he goeth upon the ground. They sleep in the trees, and build shelters from the rain. They feed upon fruit they find in the woods and upon nuts, for they eat no kind of flesh. They cannot speak, and have no more understanding than a beast.

Gorillas remained the stuff of rumour and myth until 1847 when Lowland gorillas were officially described by missionary Thomas Savage using a couple of skulls[13] and skeleton he bought from local Gabonese hunters for $25. Savage never saw a live gorilla but created his remarkably accurate description (with his co-discoverer Harvard anatomist Jeffries Wyman) of the animal through thorough interviews with local people who had observed the beast.

The sub-species the mountain gorilla was discovered in 1902 when a German soldier, Captain Robert von Beringe, shot and killed two gorillas in German East Africa and sent one specimen back to Germany to be dissected and classified.

Hippopotamus

The Strange Adventures of Andrew Battell of Leigh, in Angola and the Adjoining Regions as featured in *Purchas his Pilgrimage* (1613) contains this short but sweet account of a hippo:

Moreover, there are great store of sea or river horses, which feed always on the land, and live only by grass, and they be very dangerous in the

---

13 Two of the skulls are preserved in Harvard's Museum of Comparative Zoology. A male and a female skull, they are the holotype specimens, which are the specimens from which the official species description is created.

water. They are the biggest creature in this country, except the elephant. They have great virtue in the claws of their left forefoot, and have four claws on every foot, like the claws of an ox.

Loris

Many of the accounts of animals contained in this book are from the first impressions of an explorer rather than a naturalist and thus they may not have been able to 'name' what they saw. Indeed sometimes the animal could not be named because it was at the time of description unknown to European science.

The following extract from *A New Account of East India and Persia being Nine Years Travels 1672–1681* (1698) by John Fryer likely contains the first recorded European sighting of an Indian slow or slender loris,[14] a species that was not formally described until the mid-eighteenth century.

———————

14 A bit of detective work indicates that both the slow and slender loris have no tail, a round owl-like face and a well-developed index finger. They are also native to India.

Woods are every where, in which sometimes are met Inhabitants not yet mentioned for their Solitariness called Men of the Woods, or more truly Satyrs ... A Couple of the former I saw asleep in the day-time, in the Night they Sport and Eat; they were both in a Parrot-Cage, they had Heads like an owl, Bodied like a Monkey, without Tails; only the first Finger of the Right Hand was armed with a Claw like a Birds, otherwise they had Hands and Feet which they walk upright on, not pronely, as the other Beasts do; they were coloured like a Fox, of the length of Half a Yard; though they grow bigger till twelve Years old, when they copulate.

Flying fish

The following descriptions of flying fish are especially charming as they each use a novel way of illustrating the distance the fish can fly. The first observation took place near Tunisia and was recorded in *The Travels of Four Englishmen and a Preacher into Africa, Asia, Troy, Bythinia, Thracia, and to the Blacke Sea* (1612) by William Biddulph:

About these parts we saw flying fishes, as big as an Hearing [herring?],
with two great finnes like unto winges before, and two lesse behind; who
being chased by Dolphins and Bonitaes, fly as long as their wings are
wet, which is not farre, but oft a gables length.

This next was espied in Persia and included in *A Voyage Round the*
World (1700) by Dr John Francis Gemelli Careri:

That Day I first saw the flying fish which the Portuguese call Aquador.
It flew for about a Musket shot above the Water, and then dropt, the little
Wings not being able to support its weight of ten or twelve ounces. He
leaves his natural element to save his Life; because Abnus, or Dorado as
the Portuguese call it, continually pursues to devour it.

Terrifying fish

Spare a thought for poor Fernão Mendes Pinto (*c.* 1509–1583) who
had endured many shipwrecks on his travels. In his *The Voyages*
and Adventures of Ferdinand Mendez Pinto (published in English in
1692) Pinto tells of his experience in the seas around China and the
terrifying fish he there encountered (it is difficult to assess if these
are accurate descriptions of real animals or the product of a fevered
imagination, stoked by myth and superstition):

After we had gone from this Haven, we sailed long the Coast above thir-
teen days together, always in sight of land, and at length arrived at a
Port called Buxipalem, in the height of forty-nine Degrees. We found this
Climate somewhat colder than the rest, here we saw an infinite company
of Fishes and Serpents of such strange forms, as I cannot speak of them
without fear; Similau told Antonio de Faria incredible things concern-
ing them, as well as what he had seen himself, having been there before,
as of that had been reported to him, especially in the full Moons of the
moneths of November, December and January, when storms reign there
most, as indeed this Chinese made it appear to our own eyes, whereby

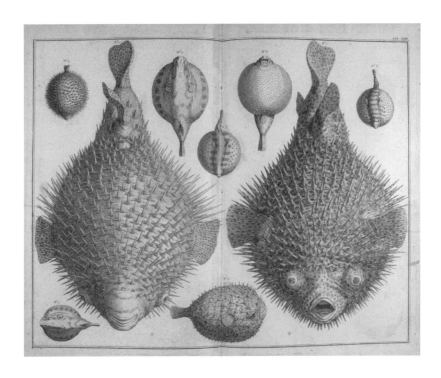

he justified unto us the most of that which he had affirmed. For in this
place we saw Fishes, in the shape of Thornbacks, that were four fathoms
about, and had a Muzzle like an Ox; likewise we saw others resembling
great Lizards, spotted all over with green and black, having three rows
of prickles on their backs, that were very sharp, and of the bigness of
an arrow; their bodies also were full of the like, but they were neither
so long, nor so great as the others: These Fishes would ever and anon
bristle themselves like Porcupines, which made them very dreadful to
behold; they had snouts that were sharp and black, with two crooked
teeth out of each jaw-bone, two spans long, like the tusks of a wild Boar.
We also saw Fishes whose bodies were exceeding black, so prodigious
and great, that their heads onely were above six spans broad. I will pass
over in silence many other Fishes of sundry sorts, which we beheld in
this place, because I hold it not fit to stand upon things that are out of my
discourse; let it suffice me to say, that during two nights we stayed here

we did not think ourselves safe, by reasons of Lizards, Whales, Fishes and Serpents, which in great numbers shewed themselves to us.

Giant tortoise

Captain William Dampier, in *A New Voyage Round the* World (1699), was impressed by the giant tortoises he found in the Galapagos Islands. Unfortunately he was most impressed with their flavour:

There is no place in the world, so well stored with guanoes and land-tortoises, as these isles. The first are fat, of an extraordinary size and exceeding tame; and the land tortoises so numerous that some hundred men may subsist on them for a considerable time, being very fat and as pleasant a food as a pullet; and of such bigness, that one of them weighs 150 or 200 pounds; and are two feet to two feet six inches over the belly; whereas in any other places, I never met with any above thirty pounds weight ... There are three or four sorts of land-tortoises in the West-Indies: One is a called by the Spaniards Hackatee, which keep most in fresh water ponds; they have small legs, and long necks, and flat feet, and commonly weigh between ten and fifteen pounds. The second sort they call Tenopen, much less than the former and something rounder; but, for the rest, not unlike them, except that the shell on their backs is naturally coloured with a curious carved work. Both sorts afford very good meat, and these last delight in low marshy places, and are in vast numbers on the isle of Pines near Cuba, among the woods ... The tortoises in the Galapagos islands are in shape like the first, with long necks, and small heads; only, they are much bigger.

Turtle

For the seventeenth-century adventurer and explorer their main purpose was to claim new lands and discover resources to exploit. Unfortunately for much of the wildlife they were more frequently viewed as just another commodity. In *A Voyage to East-India: wherein some things are taken notice of...* (1655) Edward Terry is stirred by the multi-purpose turtle:

The Turtle or Torteise is one of those creatures we call Amphibia, that lives sometimes in the Sea, and sometimes on the Shore, he is marvellously fortified by Nature, dwelling (as it were) continually under a strong roof which moves with him, and covers (when he will) his whole body ... those concave shacks (like buckets, but of an Oval shape) that cover these creatures, are many of them exceeding strong, that they will bear off the weight of a cart-wheel. These Torteises increase by eggs (as I have been often told) are very good to eat, the substance within them (whether you call it flesh or fish) first boyled, and after minced with butter, tastes like buttered Veal. Their shell makes (as is very commonly known) excellent good Combes, Cups or Boxes.

Captain William Dampier in *A New Voyage Round the* World (1699) takes a similar view of the turtle, sharing with his readers his advice on the best-tasting breed:

Upon the shoals grow great plenty of turtle grass, which makes those channels abound in that sort of sea-tortoise, called the green turtle, or

tortoise: For you must know, that there are four or five different sorts of sea-tortoises; viz the trunk-tortoise, the logger-head, the hawksbill, and green tortoise: The first is bigger and has rounder and bigger beak than the rest; but its flesh is neither wholesome nor well tasted, any more than that of the loggerhead, which feeds on moss on rocks: It borrows its name from its large head. The hawksbill (so called from its long small mouth) is the least, and that bears the so much esteemed shell, of which they make cabinets, boxes, combs &c. in Europe: Of this shell, each has from three to four pounds, though some have less; the flesh is but indifferent, yet sometimes better than that of the loggerheads; those taken betwixt Sambellos and Porto Bello, make those who eat the flesh vomit and purge vehemently.

It is further remarkable, that the flesh of the hawksbill tortoise differs according to their food; for those that feed upon moss, among the rocks, have a much yellower fat and flesh, and not so well tasted as those that feed upon grass; besides that their shells are not so transparent.

Panda

Unsurprisingly some now famous animals which inhabit remote areas or are shy of habit managed to escape the attention of European explorers for hundreds of years. The panda is a classic example. Now the image of a panda is so ubiquitous it is difficult to imagine that only 150 years ago no one in Europe had ever set eyes on one.

The first person to bring the panda to the attention of Europe was Catholic priest and naturalist Armand David (1826–1900), who spent many years in China observing and collecting the flora and fauna. Recorded in his book *Abbé David's Diary* (1870) are his efforts to secure a specimen of this 'new' bear to send back to Paris for classification:

Upon returning from an excursion we are invited to rest at the home of a certain Li, the principal landowner in the valley, who serves us tea and sweets. At this Pagan's I see a fine skin of the famous white and black bear [*Ailuropoda melanoleucus*], which appears to be fairly large. It is a remarkable species and I am delighted when I hear my hunters say that I shall certainly obtain the animal within a short time.

My Christian hunters return today after a ten-day absence. They bring me a young white bear, which they took alive but unfortunately killed so it could be carried more easily. The young white bear, which they sell to me very dearly, is all white except for the legs, ears, and around the eyes, which are deep black. The colours are the same as those I saw in the skin of an adult bear the other day at the home of Li, the hunter. This must be a new species of Ursus, very remarkable not only because of its colour, but also for its paws, which are hairy underneath, and for other characters.

They bring me a white bear which they tell me is fully adult. Its colours are exactly like those of the young one I have, only the darker parts are less black and the white more soiled. The animal's head is very big, and the snout round and short instead of being pointed as it is in the Pekin bear.

David sent back the skin to the Muséum National d'Histoire Naturelle in Paris where it was used to provide the first formal description of the new species. A live panda was not seen by Europeans until 1916 when German zoologist Hugo Weigold bought a panda cub from some locals, but unfortunately the cub died shortly after. In the 1920s the two sons of President Theodore Roosevelt; Kermit and Theodore Jr.; went on an expedition with the Chicago Field Museum and became the first Westerners to shoot a wild panda. The skin of the female they shot was sent back to America where it was widely exhibited.

Narwhal

The narwhal seems to have been known (if not named) since early in the seventeenth century. Samuel Purchas mentions the narwhal in his discussion on unicorns in *Purchas his Pilgrimage or Relations of the World* (1613):

The fish the Islanders call Narwall, which has the horn, or tooth call'd the Vnicorns horn

As for the Unicorne we have before observed, That no one beene seene these hundred yeeres last past, by testimonie of any probably Authour ... A Physician testifieth of the common Unicornes horne, that it is inferior to the Hart's horne in efficacie against poysons; and therefore not likely to bee it. I could bee of the opinion that the hornes in Venice and other places kept as jewels, are of the Sea Unicorne, a fish which has a horne in the forehead or nose thereof. Linschoten thinks the Rhinoceros is the onely Unicorne. That the Rhinoceros is onely male and the Vulture onely female, as Baubinus sheweth, many Authours conceit, is not only absurd but impious to behold.

Captain Luke Foxe (1586–1635) observed and described what we now know to be a narwhal in his 1635 book *North-West Fox or Fox from the North-west Passage*:

We remained betwixt ice and ice S, Westward, until we got cleare, in which time came under the sheering of our head (easie to have been strooke, if our provisions had beene ready) a Sea Unicorne. He was of a length about 9 foot, black ridged, with a small fin thereon, his taile stood crosse his ridge, and indented between the pickends, as it were in either side with 2 scallop shells, his side dappled purely with white and blacke, his belly all milke white, his shape from his gils to his taile was fully like a Makarell, his head like to a Lobster, wherout the fore-part grewe forth his twined horne above 6 foote long all black save the tip.

The narwhal was 'officially' discovered in 1648 when scientist
Nicolas Tulpius dissected an example that had washed up on British
shores.

Turaco

The Turaco is a brightly coloured bird native to sub-Saharan Africa.
Their plumage was much sought after as illustrated by this anec-
dote contained in *A Voyage to New South Wales* (1796) by George
Barrington, who hunted the bird in South Africa:

In searching for the Touraco, which Monsieur my master had shot, he
fell into a pit upwards of twelve feet deep, which had been dug by the
Hottentots, to entrap wild beasts, particularly the elephant. Fortunately
the hole was empty, and he had the good fortune to escape being impaled
alive on the pointed stakes fixed at the bottom of these pits: they are gener-
ally slightly covered over with slender branches of trees, and interstices
filled with turf and moss; the roots most anxiously sought after by the
elephants are strewed on the surface, and the unwieldy animal eagerly
pressing forward after his favourite food, is easily entrapped by the wily
Hottentot into the snare: being wounded by his fall he is soon dispatched.

After many fruitless efforts to extricate himself, I being at some
distance with the Hottentots, he fired his susee, and by that means
brought us back to his assistance. This accident, however serious, did
not prevent him pursuing the wounded bird, which at length he found,
and considered the acquisition as a full compensation for all his perils.
The Touraco is as agreeable in its form, as in the sweetness and melody
of its notes; it is of a bright green, a tuft of the same colour, bordered with
white, adorns its head; its eyes a sparkling red, with a streak over them
of the most dazzling white; its wings are a beautiful purple, varying to
the violet, according to the point of light in which it is viewed. It is reck-
oned by the naturalists a species of the Cuckoo; but they have been much
mistaken, as it has not the least affinity with that bird. The Cuckoo, in
every part of the world, subsists on snails and insects, but the Touraco

is fruvigorous. In whatever part of the world the Cuckoo may be, it is remarkable that she never builds a nest, but lays her eggs in those of other birds, and by this means saves herself the trouble of rearing her young; the Touraco, on the contrary, is careful of its family, builds a nest and hatches her own eggs: this difference in disposition is, I think, a sufficient reason to prove them a particular species.

Ostrich, cassowary & rhea

The Adventures of Mr T. S. an English Merchant Taken Prisoner by the Turks of Algiers (1670) contains this description of an ostrich:

There is here a great number of Ostriches; it is a notable bird, that runs and flies very speedily; no Creature is able to keep pace with it. Many extraordinary things are reported of it. The Countrey people say that they do sometimes find their Nests in the Sands: They make them in this manner; they scrape a round Pit as large as their body, where they place their Eggs in order. They lay above a hundred before they cause them to bring forth, not in a heap, but in several ranks; the sun-beams warm them and cause them to burst forth into birds; the Mother-Ostrich over-looks them, and when the first laid Eggs are become birds, she takes the farthermost Eggs to feed them until they come of age and strength to walk alone. It is a Creature that is careless of her Fruit until they are birds, and then she nourishes them with care, giving equally to all, shewing thereby her Justice. She is a bird very temperate, content with a small quantity of food, and able to digest the hardest substance, as Iron, Steel, and Stones.

The idea that an ostrich could eat hard substances seems to come from the fact that because ostriches have no teeth they tend to swallow small stones which assist the gizzard in grinding up food. In *Purchas his Pilgrimage or Relations of the World* (1613) Samuel Purchas describes another large bird, the *emia*, which is likely to have been a cassowary rather than an emu as emu are only native to Australia (which though 'discovered' by the Dutch navigator Willem

Janszoon in 1606 had yet to be explored by Europeans) and the bird he describes is native to Indonesia:

In Banda and other Islands, the bird called Emia or Eme, is admirable. It is foure foot high, somewhat resembling an Ostrich, but having three clawes on the feete, and the same exceeding strong: it hath two wings, rather to helpe it running, then serviceable for flight: the legges great and long: they say it hath no tongue, and that it putteth out the pisle [penis] backwards, as the camel: that it devoureth Orange and Egges, rendring that same in the ordure, nothing altered. It strikes with the heels like a Horse, will swallow an Apple whole as big as ones fist, yea, it swalloweth downe burning coals without harme, and in a contrary extreme, pieces of ice.

In *An Account of a Voyage up the River de la Plata and Thence Over Land to Peru* (1698), Acarete du Biscay describes the rhea (a bird from the ostrich family, native to South America):

There are likewise abundance of Ostriches who herd in Flocks like Cattle, and tho' they are good Meat, yet none but the Savages eat of them. They make Umbrellas of their Feathers, which are very commodious in the Sun; their Eggs are good and every body eats of 'em, tho' they say they are hard of digestion. I saw one of these Creatures very remarkable, and that is, while the Hen sits upon the Eggs, they have the Instinct or foresight to provide for their Young; so five or six days before they come out of the Shell, they set an Egg in each of the four corners of the place where they sit, these Eggs they break, and when they rot, Worms and Maggots breed in 'em in prodigious numbers, which serve to nourish the Young Ostriches from the time they are hatch'd till they are able to go further for their sustenance.

Du Biscay's keen observation of the rhea's nest is fairly accurate. The polygamous males build the nest in which all his females lay their eggs. He then places a number of eggs outside the nest to act as decoys, in the hope that predators will make off with the sacrificed eggs and leave the actual nest alone.

Dodo

The dodo has become something of an emblem of man's negative impact on nature. The dodo, native to Mauritius, was first described by Dutch travellers in 1598 and the last recorded sighting of the enigmatic creature was in 1662, the poor flightless bird having been hunted to extinction. This account comes from *Some Years Travels into Africa & Asia* by Sir Thomas Herbert (1677, 4th ed.) who first wrote of his experiences in 1634 in the first edition of his book. This extract is from the fourth and final edition, to which he made some retrospective changes:

The Dodo, a bird the Dutch call Walgh-vogel or Dod Eersen: her body is round and fat which occasions the slow pace or that her corpulence; and so great as few of them weighs less than fifty pound: meat it is with some, but better to the eye than stomach; such as only a strong appetite can vanquish: but otherwise, through its olyness it cannot chuse but quickly cloy and nauseate the stomach, being indeed more pleasurable to look upon then feed upon. It is of a melancholy visage, as sensible of Natures injury in framing so massive a body to be directed by comple- mental wings, such indeed as are unable to hoise her from the ground, serving only to rank her amongst Birds: her head is variously drest. For one half is hooded with down of a dark colour; the other half naked and of a white hue, as if Lawn were drawn over it; her bill hooks and bends downwards, the trill or breathing place is in the midst from which part to the end, the colour is of a light green mixt with a pale yellow: her eyes are round and bright, and instead of feathers has a most fine down; her train (like to a Chyna beard) is no more than three or four short feathers: her legs are thick and black; her tallons great; her stomach fiery, so as she can easily digest stones.

The following account in *Voyage from New South Wales to Canton in the year 1788* by Thomas Gilbert (1789) does not concern the dodo, but it does illustrate the plight of the birds living on uninhabited islands who were easy pickings for hungry sailors:

Great numbers of gannets, very large and fat, were walking with less fear and concern than geese in a farm yard; and they were taken by hand, with much more ease. We found their nests in the long grass at the head of the beach, in each of which there were a great number of eggs, very large, and well tasted when dressed. On entering the woods I was surprised to see large fat pigeons, of the same plumage and make as those in Europe, sitting on low bushes, and so insensible to fear, as to be knocked down with little trouble. Partridges likewise, in great plenty, ran along the ground, very fat, and exceedingly well tasted. Several of those I knocked down, and their legs being broken, I placed them near me as I sat under a tree. The pain they suffered caused them to make a doleful cry, which brought five or six dozen of the same kind to them, and by that means I was able to take nearly the whole of them. I might not

otherwise have procured so many; for, although they were by no means shy, yet they ran very fast when chased.

Cat

First encounters go both ways, as this delightful account from *A New Voyage and Description of the Isthmus of America* by Lionel Wafer (1699) proves:

They are exceedingly pester'd with Mice and Rats, which are mostly Grey; and a Brood of Cats therefore to destroy these, might be as acceptable a Present to them as better Dogs for their Hunting. When I left the Isthmus, 2 of the Indians who came aboard the same vessel at the Samballoe's, went a Cruising with us towards the Corn-Islands and Cartagene: And when they were dispos'd to return, and we were studying to oblige 'em with some present, one of them spied a Cat we had aboard, and beg'd it: Which we had no sooner given him, but he and his Consort, without staying for any other Gift, went immediately into their Canoa, and paddled off with abundance of Joy. They had learnt the use of Cats while they were aboard.

Palmeiras ofte Palmboomen,
daer die Indiaensche nooten aen
waschen genaemt Coquos.

Chauderin

Bayleo

Cocco

Lanha

Cocco   Uyghen blat.

FOOD, FRUIT & PLANTS

Encounters with food – world cuisine

As any modern traveller will agree, one of the chief delights of travelling to far-flung corners of the globe is to taste the local food. This was no different for our early explorers, except that they were coming from a Europe where plain food was the norm and the diet was limited to seasonal produce. Thus tasting spices and experiencing new textures and flavours would have carried a much bigger impact.

John Mocquet in *Travels and Voyages into Africa, Asia and America, the East and West-Indies; Syria, Jerusalem and the Holy-Land* (1696) describes the food of Morocco:

> *As for the Couscoussou of which I have made mention, and which I have Tasted several times, it is Meal made up and Kneaded into the fashion of Sugar-Plums or Comfits, with Water, in a Frying-pan; then put it in an Earthern Vessel full of holes at the bottom, like a Cullender; after that, it is put in a Pot upon a hot Fire, and the Vapour boils it; then they pour Broth there-upon, and eat it by great bits like Balls: It is of a very good Taste, which nourishes and fattens the Body to Admiration.*

In *A Short Journey in the West Indies in which are interspersed Curious Anecdotes and Characters* (1790) the author vividly describes a mouth-watering meal he was treated to in the West Indies:

The dinner being served, we sat down to a table that was plentifully, and not inelegantly covered, doing great credit to Benniba's taste. In the middle stood an excellent pepper-pot. I must describe this dish – it is an olio, consisting of a large piece of mess beef, boiled to rags; a number of the leaves of toyau calliloo, a vegetable, I believe, peculiar to the torrid zone; some pods of negro pepper, with a quantity of another peculiar vegetable, called ocro, with thyme and scallions; to this is added crabs, shrimps, and cray-fish in abundance; and it is further thickened with dough dumplings and yams: the prevailing colour is green, through which we see rising the red of the cray-fish and shrimps, the white of the dumplings and yams, and the various hues of different peppers. When well made, as was that I am describing, it is a very tempting dish.

William Biddulph recounts the food he tasted in Turkey in *The Travels of Four Englishmen and a Preacher into Africa, Asia, Troy, Bythinia, Thracia, and to the Blacke Sea* (1612):

The diet of the Turks is not very sumptuous, for the most common dish is Pilaw, which is good savourie meat, made of Rice and small morsels of Mutton boiled therein, and sometimes roasted Buckbones (that is small bits or morsels of flesh). Their more costly fare is Sambouse and Muclebits. Sambouses are made of paste like a great round Pastie, with varieties of hearbes and meats therein, not minced but in Buckbones. A Muclebite is a dish made of Egges and hearbes.

John Saris (*c.* 1580–1643) recorded the food of Japan in *The Voyage of John Saris to Japan* (1613):

The dyet used generally through the Countrey is Rice of divers sorts, one better then other (as our Wheate and Corne here), the whitest accounted the best, which they use in stead of Bread: Fish, fresh and salted; some pickled Herbes, Beanes, Raddishes and other Roots salted and pickled; Wild-fowle, Ducke, Mallard, Teale, Geese, Pheasant, Partridge, Quaile, and divers others, which they doe powder and put up in pickle. Of Hens

they have great store, as likewise Deere both red and fallow; wild Bores, Hares, Goates, Kine, etc. Of Cheese[15] they have plentie. Butter they make none, neither will they eate any Milke, because they hold it to bee as bloud, nor tame beasts.

Of tame Swine and Pigs they have great abundance. Wheate they have as good as any of ours, being red. They plow both with Oxen and Horse as wee doe heere ... The ordinarie drinke of the common people is water, which with their meate they drinke warme, holding it to bee a sovereigne remedie against Wormes in the maw: other drinkes they have none, but what is distilled out of Rice, which is almost as strong as our Aquavitae, and in colour like to Canarie Wine, and is not deare.

Medieval Flemish Franciscan missionary William of Rubruck (1220–1293) detailed the diet of the Mongols in *The Journey to the Eastern Parts of the World by Friar William of Rubruck 1253–55*:

---

15 It seems likely that the author is referring to tofu or bean curd here as cheese has never been part of the Japanese diet.

Of their food and victuals you must know that they eat all their dead animals without distinction, and with such flocks and herds it cannot be but that many animals die. Nevertheless, in summer, so long as lasts their cosmos, that is to say mare's milk, they care not for any other food. So then if it happens that an ox or a horse dies, they dry its flesh by cutting it into narrow strips and hanging it in the sun and the wind, where at once and without salt it becomes dry without any evil smell. With the intestines of horses they make sausages better than pork ones, and they eat them fresh. The rest of the flesh they keep for winter. With the hides of oxen they make big jars, which they dry in admirable fashion in the smoke. With the hind part of the hide of horses they make most beautiful shoes. With the flesh of a single sheep they give to eat to L [50] men or C [100]; for they cut it up very fine in a platter with salt and water, for they make no other sauce; and then with the point of a knife or a fork which they make for the purpose, like that which we use to eat coddled pears or apples, they give each of the bystanders a mouthful or two according to the number of guests.

The staple of the Mongolian diet was cosmos, or mare's milk. Here Rubruck describes how it is made:

This cosmos, which is mare's milk, is made in this wise. They stretch a long rope on the ground fixed to two stakes in the ground, and to this rope they tie toward the third hour the colts of the mares they want to milk. Then the mothers stand near their foal, and allow themselves to be quietly milked; and if one be too wild, then a man takes the colt and brings it to her, allowing it to suck a little, then he takes it away and the milker takes its place. When they have got together a great quantity of milk, which is sweet as cow's as long as it is fresh, they pour it into a big skin or bottle, and they set to churning it with a stick prepared for that purpose, and which is as big as a man's head at its lower extremity and hollowed out; and when they have beaten it sharply it begins to boil up like new wine and to sour or ferment, and they continue to churn it until they have extracted the butter. Then they taste it, and when it is mildly pungent, they drink it. It is pungent on the tongue like rapé wine when drunk, and when a man has finished drinking, it leaves a taste of milk of almonds on the tongue, and it makes the inner man most joyful and also intoxicates weak heads, and greatly provokes urine.

The diet in seventeenth-century Bangladesh was described in *Travels of Fray Sebastien Manrique 1629–1643*:

Their daily meal consists of rice with which, if they have nothing else to add, they take salt and are satisfied. They also use a kind of herb which is usually call Xaga [sag in Hindi, greens or spinach]: those better off use milk, ghī, and other lacteous preparations: fish is little eaten, especially by those who live inland. The flesh of certain animals is also used, such as goats, kids and castrated goats known as Bacari flesh. Besides this wild pig or jabalis, wild pigeon, doves, quail and other similar living things are eaten, but in no circumstances do they touch tame pig, hens, eggs, or the flesh of other tame animals, especially of cows or oxen.

There are, however, among these unbelievers and pagans some strict sects whose followers not only refuse to eat any living thing, but will not even touch vegetables if they are of a red colour, as they say that to eat anything of the colour of blood is borō gunā, which means "great sin". This sect of Idolators usually eats kachari, a dish made of rice mixed with lentils, it may be added, of two parts rice to one of lentils, or instead of the latter Mungo, a vegetable of no great size of a dark green colour, very digestible and good for sick people. To these ingredients they add a large quantity of ghī so as to give it body.

The food of Ceylon (Sri Lanka) is discussed in *Francois Valentijn's Descriptions of Ceylon* (1724):

Rice is their bread and they are satisfied if they have some salt, a little stewed vegetables with pepper and salt added and some lemon juice over it. To eat beef is a crime among them. There is not much of other flesh or fish and if they have some they will rather make money and sell it to foreigners than eat it themselves, but for the very important and the noblemen who have on their tables various curries of fish or flesh steamed for a long time. For otherwise it is an honour among them to be sparing, miserly and stingy and those who know how to subsist very frugally are often praised.

Dr John Francis Gemelli Careri in *A Voyage Round the World* (1700) was somewhat puzzled by Chinese eating habits:

The Chinese generally drink hot, and eat cold, just contrary to the Europeans; nor will any of them ever refresh their palates with Cold Water, tho' the weather be never so hot, or they droughty with travelling; but wait patiently until they have it so hot it scalds their Lips.

Among the Mandarines and the great ones; who tho' they furnish their tables with Birds Nests which cost 300 pieces of Eight a measure, the Fins of Sharks, the Sinews of Stags, precious Roots and other things of great Value, yet they prate so long all goes cold.

Pineapple

Pineapples are indigenous to South America and because they are easily transplanted and cultivated the pineapple quickly spread throughout the tropics. Traders and colonialists from Portugal introduced the Brazilian pineapple into India in the 1550s and the Spanish took the pineapple to the Philippines and Hawaii in the early eighteenth century.

Pineapples were first noted by a European in 1493 when no less than Christopher Columbus found one in Guadeloupe and brought a sample back to Europe. Sugar at this time was still a rarity and fresh fruit was only available for limited periods when in season so the incredible sweetness of the pineapple ensured its enduring popularity.

Dutch colonialists cultivated the pineapples they found in Surinam and brought many back to Europe. In 1658, Dutch economist Pieter de la Court was credited as the first European to successfully grow a pineapple in Europe. The elaborate and costly hot houses required to raise the tropical fruit in our colder climes meant that pineapples became the preserve of the rich and wealthy and were seen as a status symbol – as attested by the frequent imagery of the pineapple in art[16] and architecture of the period.

Such was the cachet of the pineapple that it was said hostesses would frequently re-use a pineapple as part of a table display until it rotted. Others rented a pineapple for their dinner party as a centre-piece and returned it uneaten to be used again and again. Only the very rich could afford to actually eat the fruit – King Louis XV ate a pineapple grown at Versailles in 1793. In this way the pineapple became a symbol of hospitality, especially in America, where it was frequently used as a motif on public buildings and lavish homes to indicate the hospitality offered within.

Samuel Purchas related travellers' experience of the pineapple in India in *Purchas his Pilgrimage or Relations of the World* (1613):

Of their fruits, Ananas [pineapple] is reckoned to be one of the best: in taste like an Apricocke, in shew a farre off like an Artichoke, but without prickles, very sweet of scent. It was first brought out of the West Indies hither: it is as great as a Melon; the juyce thereof is like sweet Must.

John Fryer tells of the pineapples he tried in India in *A New Account of East India and Persia being Nine Years Travels 1672–1681* (1698):

The Fruit the English call a Pine-Apple (the Moors, Ananas) because of the resemblance, cuts within as firm as a pippin; Seedy, if not fully ripe; the Taste inclinable to Tartness, though most excellently qualified by a dulcid Sapor that imposes upon the Imagination and Gustative Faculty

---

16 A 1675 painting by Hendrick Danckerts depicts King Charles II being presented with the first pineapple to be grown in England, indicating the strong symbolism and prestige afforded by the royal privilege of tasting the fruit.

a Fancy that it relishes of any Fruit a Man likes, and some will swear
it: It grows thick on a Stalk like an Artichoke, emitting a Tuft of Leafs
upon the Crown ... the Juice will corrode any Iron or Knife, like Limon.

Equally impressed by the flavour was Edward Terry in *A Voyage to East-India: wherein some things are taken notice of...* (1655):

And to conclude with the best of all other their choyce Fruits, the Ananas, like unto our Pine-Apples, which seems to the taster to be a most pleasing compound made of Strawberries, Claret-wine, Rose-water and Sugar well tempered together.

A True and Faithful Account of What was Observed in Ten Years Travells into the Principal Places of Europe, Asia, Africa and America by R. F. Esq (1665) contain this account of a pineapple tasted in Brazil:

But above all, the Ananaz is one of the deliciousest Plants the Earth did e'er produce, it growing like an Artichoke, the leaves thick and sharply indented, like those of Sempervive,[17] thriftly on the top, with a rind all scaly like the pine-apple, which paring off you find the fruit of the bignesse of an ordinary meloon, of a Golden colour, and distinguished into Cells, like Oranges, which slicing and eating in wine (as 'twas affirm'd of Manna) every one finds that gust and tast in't, he is the most delighted with.

A New Voyage and Description of the Isthmus of America by Lionel Wafer (1699) is equally effusive about the fruit:

On the Isthmus grows that delicious Fruit which we call the Pine-Apple, in shape not much unlike an Artichoke, and as big as a Man's Head. It grows like a Crown on the top of a Stalk about as big as ones Arm, and a Foot and a half high. The Fruit is ordinarily about six Pound weight; and is inclos'd with short prickly Leaves like an Artichoke. They do not strip, but pare off

---

17 Succulent plants from the *Crassulaceae* family, more commonly known as house-leeks.

these Leaves to get at the Fruit; which hath no Stone or Kernel in it. 'Tis very juicy; and some fancy it resemble the Tast of all the most delicious Fruits one can imagine mixd together. It ripens at all times of the Year, and is rais'd from new Plants.

By 1788 Europeans had begun growing pineapples at home as *An Abridgement of Captain Cook's First and Second Voyages* (1788) reveals:

Pine-apples grow here [Batavia, Dutch Indonesia] in such abundance, that they may be purchased, at the first hand, for the value of an English farthing; and they bought some very large ones for a halfpenny a piece at the fruit-shops. Though they are excellent eating, it is imagined they are reared to equal perfection in the hot-houses of England. They grow so luxuriantly, that seven or eight suckers have been seen adhering to one item.

It is interesting to note the similar frame of reference with which many of the explorers use to describe the pineapple – likening it in shape to an artichoke. This in itself is notable as the artichoke, native to the Mediterranean, only reached the Netherlands and England in the sixteenth century and so was a relatively new arrival itself.

Sago

Sago is a starch harvested from the centre of the Sago palm (*Metroxylon sagu* and *Metroxylon rumphii*) which is native to the Southwest Pacific and is a staple foodstuff there.

Sago became popular as an 'invalid' food in Britain in Victorian times and, like tapioca, was commonly used as a pudding in the early twentieth century (much to the horror of school children, who frequently compared the jellified balls of sago pearls to frogspawn).

In *A Voyage to New Guinea* (1779) Captain Thomas Forrest (*c.* 1729–*c.* 1802) describes the process of extracting and using the sago in Gilolo, Maluku Islands, Indonesia:

The sago or libby tree, has, like the coconut tree, no distinct bark that peels off, and may be defined as a long tube of hard wood, about two inches thick, containing a pulp or pith mixed with many longitudinal fibres. The tree being felled, it is cut into lengths of about five or six feet. A part of the hard wood is then sliced off, and the workman, coming to the pith, cuts across (generally with an adze made of hard wood called aneebong) the longitudinal fibres and the pith together; leaving a part at each end uncut; so that, when it is excavated, there remains a trough, into which the pulp is again put, mixed with water, and beat with a piece of wood; then the fibres separated from the pulp, float atop, and the flour subsides. After being cleared in this manner by several waters, the pulp is put into cylindrical baskets, made of the leaves of the tree; and, if it is to be kept some time, those baskets are generally sunk in fresh water.

One tree will produce from two to four hundred weight of flour ... The Papua oven, for this flour, is made of earthen ware ... Whilst the oven is heating, the baker, is supposed to have prepared his flour, by breaking the lumps small; moistening it with water, if too dry, and passing it once or twice through a sieve, at the same time rejecting any parts that look black or smell sour. This done, he fills the cells with the flour, lays a bit of clean leaf over, then covers all up with leaves, and puts a stone or piece of wood atop, to keep in the heat. In about ten or twelve minutes, the cakes will be sufficiently baked according to their thickness; and bread thus baked, will keep, I am told, several years. I have kept it twelve months, nor did vermin destroy it in that time.

The sago bread, fresh from the oven, eats just like hot rolls. I grew very fond of it, as did both my officers ... A sago cake, when hard, requires to be soaked in water, it then softens and swells into a curd, like biscuit soaked; but, if eat without soaking (unless fresh from the oven) it feels disagreeable, like sand in the mouth.

Mango

Mangos are native to South and Southeast Asia, and from here traders and explorers helped the fruit to spread throughout the tropics.

Pepper Tree

Sagou Fruit

Pepper Fruit

The Portuguese were the first Europeans to establish a trade in mangos after they arrived in Calcutta in 1498. The Spanish then introduced mangos to Mexico and South America in the seventeenth century and the fruit flourished in tropical climes.

The difficulty of cultivating the plant outside of the tropics and the problematic issue of transporting the soft fruit long distances meant that the mango did not reach a wider European audience until the twentieth century.

In *Travels of Fray Sebastien Manrique 1629–1643* the Portuguese explorer is enchanted by his first taste of a mango in India:

This superabundance of dainties was augmented by a variety of fruits, specially of mangoes, a fruit so choice and delectable that, had the old rhymers or Poets known of it, no doubt they would have given it a place above all the nectars and ambrosias of their dream-gods. Exaggeration apart, I maintain that good mangoes can hold their own with the choicest fruits of our Europe. The form is generally oval, but some are quite round: at its largest it equals the head of a two or three years old child, while the smallest are of the size of a goose's egg. The colour tends rather to a deep than a pale green, while in some the colour is a charming mixture of pale yellow and pink, which makes them most beautiful to look at. These last have a most pleasing and delicate fragrance. The interior of the fruit consists of a straw-coloured yellow pulp, enclosed in a thick skin, much tougher than that of an apple, which must be thrown aside to enable one to eat down to the stone, which too has to be thrown away.

Edward Terry suggests a rather novel way of eating the mango in *A Voyage to East-India: wherein some things are taken notice of...* (1655):

Another most excellent fruit they have, called a Manggo, growing upon Trees as big as our walnut-trees, and as these here, so those trees there, will be very full of that most excellent Fruit, in shape and colour like unto our Apricocks, but much bigger; which taken and rolled in a man's hands when they are thorough ripe, the substance within them becomes like the pap of roasted Apple, which when suck'd out from about a large stone they have within them, is delicately pleasing unto every Palate that tastes it.

Dr John Francis Gemelli Careri in *A Voyage Round the World* (1700) is rather less effusive regarding the charms of the mango:

The Manguera or Mango-Tree is as high as a good Pear-Tree, but has large softer Leaves. The Mango it bears is weighty and flat, and hangs downwards by a long Stalk. Without they are green, and the Pulp within the Shell is white and yellow.

But John Fryer makes up for Careri's rather factual description with a glowing account in *A New Account of East India and Persia being Nine Years Travels 1672–1681*:

The mango (which they have improved in all its kinds to the utmost Perfection) being a Sovereign Medicine; they are the best and largest in India, most like a Pear-Plum, but three times as big, grow on a Tree nearest a Plum-Tree; the Fruit when Green scents like Turpentine, and pickled are the best Achars to provoke an Appetite; when ripe the Apples of Hisperides are but Fables to them; for Taste, the Nectarine, Peach, and Apricot fall short.

Prickly pear

The prickly pear is actually the fruit from a cactus (*Opuntia ficus-indica*). It grows in arid regions of Mexico, South America, North Africa and the Middle East. The small flowers atop the cactus form into small round fruits which are most often used to make jellies, jams and sweets.

In *The Adventures of Mr T. S. an English Merchant Taken Prisoner by the Turks of Algiers* (1670) the writer comes across some prickly pears in North Africa:

Here is a strange sort of Tree made up of Leaves, one Leaf grows on the top of another; the Leaves are thick two or three inches in the middle; they are above a foot large and long; an excellent Fruit grows upon them, which the Arabs call Asholoch, our English, Prickle Pear; the Substance is cold and refreshing; it is ripe about Midsummer, and of a yellowish

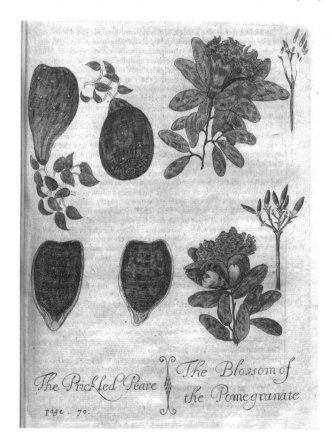

colour. Every Garden is furnished with such a Tree: The Rind is full of
little Prickles undiscernible; therefore it is not to be handled with naked
hands. I have since seen some in other parts.

Captain William Dampier in *A New Voyage Round the World* (1699)
discovered that eating lots of the fruit had an interesting side-effect:

The prickly pear grows upon a shrub five feet high, in many places in the
West-Indies. It thrives best in saltish sandy grounds, near the sea-shore.
Each branch of this shrub has two or three round leaves, of the breadth
of a man's hand, not unlike houseleek [see p.102], edged with prickles an
inch long. At the extremity of the leaf grows the fruit, the bigness of a
large plum, small towards, the leaf and thicker to the end, where it opens
like a medlar. The fruit has also small prickles, and is green at first, but
turns red by degrees. The pulp is of the same colour with the substance
of a thick syrup, with small black seeds. Its taste is pleasant and
cooling. I have often observed, that, if you eat twenty or more of them
at a time, they will colour the urine as red as blood; but without any
ill consequence.

Coconut

The coconut is such a multi-purpose fruit – it encompasses a drink,
within tasty flesh, within a shell that can be used as a cup or bowl,
within a husk from which rope or fabric can be fashioned. Not only
all that but it also floats, hence the coconut's great success in spreading throughout the tropics.

It is unsurprising then that the coconut has always been a favourite
with sailors (indeed it was said to have been Captain Bligh's accusa-
tion that Fletcher Christian had stolen coconuts from the Captain's
private stores that contributed to the mutiny on *HMS The Bounty*).

Edward Terry in *A Voyage to East-India: wherein some things are*
taken notice of... (1655) writes of the many uses of the coconut:

A Coco-tree *A Batt* *A Tropique bird* *A Palmeto-tree*

The Coquer-nuttree (of which this land hath abundance) of all other Trees may challenge the preheminence: for, meerly with these trees, without the least help of any other Timber, or any other thing (unless a little iron-work) a man may build, and furnish, and fit and victual a small ship to sea ... and the very large Nuts that grow upon it (of which are made excellent drinking Cups) when it is newly gathered hath a milk-white substance that is tender (tasting like an Almond) round about of a good substance within it; and within that very pleasant Liquor, that is wholsom, as well as savoury, which may for a need serve those which sail in this Ship for meat and drink.

Sir Thomas Herbert in *Some Years Travels into Africa & Asia* (1677, 4th ed.) was equally taken by the charms of the rather handy coconut:

The Coco (another excellent fruit) is covered with a thick rind, equal in bigness to a Cabbage; some resemble the shell to the skull of a man, or rather a Deaths Head; like eyes, nose and mouth ... within we find better than the out-side promised; yielding a quart of Ambrosie, coloured like new white Wine, but far more aromatick tasted; the meat or kernel like other nuts cleaves to the shell and is not easily parted; the pith or meat is above an Inch thick, and better relisht than our Philberts, enough to satiate the appetite of two reasonable men.

Christopher Fryke in *A Relation of Two Several Voyages made into the East Indies* (1700) is so impressed by the many uses of the coconut he cannot even be bothered to recount them all:

The next to this is the Coco-Nut... The Leaves of this Tree serve the Inhabitants for a common covering for their Houses, and keep them as dry as our Tiles. The stalks of them they bind together, to make Brooms; and they use hardly any thing else throughout all India. The outward Coat of the Nutt is good to make Match, which burns better than that we use in Europe. The Sap serves for Oyl to burn. The Kernel being prest, yields a Milk, of which they make a very pretty kind of Cheeses; and it is good for several other uses, as our Milk is. The Shell is good to make Cups, Spoons, &c. It would be too tedious to relate the many uses every part of this Tree is good for.

Bamboo

Bamboo originated in China where it was used in housebuilding and to make bows and arrows and other household goods. Bamboo is in fact a type of grass and as it grows and matures so quickly it has proved to be an extremely useful resource, ensuring its spread across the world.

German botanist Georg Eberhard Rumpf was one of the first Europeans to describe bamboo in his extensive 1626 book *Herbarium Amboinense,* although he referred to the 24 variants included in his book as rohrbäume (reed-trees). It was not until the mid-1700s that the noted taxonomist Linnaeus used the word 'bamboo'.

Bamboo plants were first shipped to Europe in the mid-nineteenth century and became a popular feature in botanical gardens, but were put to no practical use (although in 1894 a patent number 8274 was registered in the UK for bamboo bicycles).

In *Travels of Fray Sebastien Manrique 1629–1643* the Portuguese missionary came across bamboo in Bangladesh:

These bambus are, as I mentioned before a species of cane, much like our canes but beyond all comparison much stronger, especially those styled "male bambus".[18] Some of these are as thick as a man's leg. Those bambus which do not exceed the size of a man's arm in circumference are of great commercial value, each cane being worth from two to three hundred rupees, owing to their being in high demand as poles for palanquins.[19] These being of sufficient length can be arched in the centre, while the ends still give room for two men, one at each side. These men who bear the palanquin on their shoulders, are, as it were, the bullocks for such vehicles, and not only are they so in fact but even are so in name, as they are called bueyes throughout India.

Lychee

Dr John Francis Gemelli Careri first tasted a lychee in China and wrote his impressions in *A Voyage Round the World* (1700):

There are also ... other Fruits of a most excellent Taste. One called Naichi, or Lichie (by the Portugueses Lichias) shap'd like, and as big as a Walnut, with a thin Rind like the Scale of a Fish. Before it is ripe it is Green, and when ripe draws towards a Carnation, the Taste delicious, and so much priz'd by the Chineses, *that they keep it dry.*

---

18 Bamboos are traditionally classed as male or female; the female variety is hollow and the male has a near solid core.

19 A palanquin is a litter.

Oranges

Oranges are thought to be native to Southeast Asia and India and have been cultivated in China since 2500 BC. There are no 'wild' orange trees, as oranges are thought to be a hybrid of the pomelo[20] and mandarin. Because oranges have been cultivated for such a long time many different varieties have developed.

The bitter orange was brought to Europe from the Holy Land by crusaders in the eleventh century and the sweet orange was introduced in the late fifteenth century by Spanish and Portuguese traders.

The fruit quickly gained popularity (and cachet) in Europe and the wealthy built glasshouses (or orangeries) in order to grow oranges in our colder climate. By the mid-sixteenth century sweet oranges were familiar to most Europeans, although only the rich could afford to actually eat them.

Edward Terry in *A Voyage to East-India: wherein some things are taken notice of...* (1655) writes of the oranges he tasted in Africa:

Here we had the best Oranges that ever I tasted, which were little round ones, exceeding sweet and juicie having but a little spongie skin within them, and the rinde on them almost as thin as the paring of an Apple. We eat all together, Rinde and Juice, and found them a Fruit that was extraordinary well pleasing to the Taste.

Sir Thomas Herbert in *Some Years Travels into Africa & Asia* (1677, 4th ed.) ate oranges in India:

Orenges we had also store of; which may well be remembered they were so succulent and dainty, and of so curious a relish as affects the eater beyond measure; the rind also was no less pleasant then the juice, seeming to have dulcity and acrimony mixed together. The tree has not only blossoms, but green and ripe Fruit all at once; the root

---

20 The Pomelo *(Citrus maxima)* is a large citrus fruit of a light green colour; it has very thick rind and pith, but the segmented fruit within has a sweet flavour.

where the sap lies constantly conveying vegetation to the tree in those warm regions.

Tea

According to legend tea was first discovered by accident. In 2737 BC Chinese emperor Shen Nung was sitting beneath a tree while his servant boiled him some water to drink. As the servant was passing the emperor his beverage some leaves from a nearby *Camellia sinensis* tree blew into his cup, and as a keen herbalist Shen Nung decided to try the resultant infusion. This rather whimsical tale was said to be the start of a long history of tea-drinking in China.

Tea first came to Britain in 1658 (an advert was placed in London newspaper, *Mercurius Politicus*, announcing that a new drink 'tee' had arrived at a coffee house in Sweeting's Rents in the City); however it was ridiculously expensive and painfully hard to get hold of, making it the new status symbol. Those fortunate enough to be able to afford some tea leaves kept them locked in special tea caddies and ensured the key was always about their person. Tea was served in the tiniest of porcelain cups and was drunk by ladies in the most fashionable houses.

Thomas Twining opened his first tea shop in 1717 and the Georgians really took to tea drinking in a big way as faster and more efficient tea clippers were able to meet demand and reduce the cost.

Purchas his Pilgrimage or Relations of the World (1613) contains this description of the Chinese habit of drinking tea:

I cannot passe by some rarities; as their shrub whence they make their drinke cia. They gather the leaves in the Spring and dry them in the shadow, and keepe it for daily decoction, using it at meates, and as often as any guest comes to their house, yea twice or thrice, if hee make any tarrying. They sup it hot, bitterish to the palate, but wholesome: not an ancient use as they have no ancient Character in their books for it ... the Chinois put the leaves themselves into the hot water, which they drink, leaving the leaves behinde.

In 1637 British traveller Peter Mundy was the first Briton to describe tasting tea in China in *The Travels of Peter Mundy in Europe and Asia 1608–1667* (1667), though he was rather concise:

The people there gave us a certaine Drinke called Chaa, which is only water with a kind of herbe boyled in itt. It must bee Drancke warme and is accompted wholesome.

A Voyage Round the World by Dr John Francis Gemelli Careri (1700) describes the many health benefits ascribed to tea by the Chinese:

The Herb Tea, or Chia, being the most valu'd Drink among the Chinese, as Chocolate is among the Spaniards; because there is no visit where they do not use a great quantity of it, we will therefore say something of it. Tho' it has the name of a Herb, yet the Leaves are gathered from little Trees ... First they are little heated in a cauldron over a gentle fire, then they are laid upon a fine mat, and turn'd with the Hands; then they are

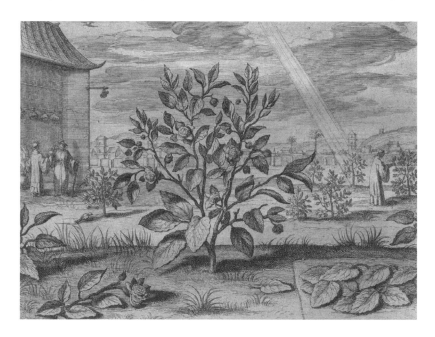

set over the fire again till they are thorough dry, and lastly they are put into wooden or tin vessels, that they may not evaporate, and be preserved from moisture. When they would make use of it, they put it into a pot, and pour boiling water over it, which extends and makes them Green as they were at first, and the water takes a pleasant scent, and a taste that is not disagreeable, especially when the leaves turn it Green. There is such variety, and so many sort of this herb, and the difference of its virtue, that there is some of it sold for about ten pence a pound and some for ten shillings. One sort makes the Water of a Gold colour, another Green; and as for the Taste some make it bitter. The best of it is very dear. The Chinese attribute it to this Herb, that neither the Gout, nor Stone are known in their Empire. They say, that taken after Dinner, it prevents indigestion, and takes away all Crudities from the Stomach; it helps Concoction, prevents Drunkeness hindring the Fumes of Wine to fly up to the Head; takes away all the uneasiness of a Surfeit, drying up, and Expelling all superfluous Humours; and helps studious Persons that desire to Watch._

Bananas & plantains

Bananas and plantains are different varieties of the same plant. In Europe we tend to see them as separate foodstuffs – the banana is for eating raw, the plantain for cooking – whereas in much of the rest of the world the two species are interchangeable.

Bananas have been domesticated for many thousands of years; the first evidence of cultivation is in Papua New Guinea from around 5000 BC. The fruit spread throughout Asia on to Africa and the Middle East. The banana was first known in Europe in Medieval times when the Moors brought them into Cyprus and Spain, but they did not reach England until the mid-seventeenth century and were not commonly eaten until Victorian times.

Today's most common variety of banana is the Cavendish banana. In 1829 Charles Telfair shipped some especially tasty banana plants he found in Mauritius back to England. They ended up in the hands of the 6th Duke of Devonshire, William Cavendish. Cavendish's gardener Joseph Paxton (who later went on to design the Crystal Palace) began to cultivate the plant in the hot houses of Chatsworth. By 1836 the Cavendish banana was formally recognised as a new cultivar and was sent back out to the Caribbean, South Pacific and Australia.

By the 1830s mass banana production in South America and the Caribbean began and the fruit became popular the world over.[21] In

21 It is said that bananas and chocolate were the foods most missed by the English during World War II rationing. Auberon Waugh remembered in his autobiography that his mother managed to source three precious bananas, one for each of her children, as a treat during the arduous war years. Auberon's father, the novelist Evelyn Waugh took hold of the bananas himself, smothered them in sugar and cream and proceeded to eat them all as his children looked on miserably.

the 1950s the Cavendish banana became the most popular variety in the world after the Gros Michel banana was nearly wiped out by Panama disease. Not bad for a variety developed in the glasshouses of Derbyshire.

A Breife Discovery or Description of the Most Famous Island of Madagascar (1646) by Richard Boothby contains this description of plantains:

> *There may be also had many other trees of excellent fruits as Mirabolins, and Plantans, which our English tearm them Apples of paradise, wherewith the Serpent beguiled Eve, the Mirabolins and Plantans from the trees are farre daintier in tast then our Apricocks, and when they are preserved, are well known to Confectioners and Phisitions, for health and pleasure. The Plantan growes by clusters as 100 or more or lesse together, as big as a large beane cod, and is so pleasant in tast, cutting it in small pieces, as parsnips to butter, men use to eate it continually at meales, with viniger, pepper and salt, to abate the sweetness, and the tree being about the bignesse of a reasonable Apple tree, beares no boughs but great leaves an ell long, or longer, and both leaves and body are excellent meat for Cowes, for the body is no harder then a well growne cabbidge, and may be cut downe by a good sword at a blow.*

Some Years Travels into Africa & Asia (1677, 4th ed.) by Sir Thomas Herbert has an account of the bananas of India:

> *The Bananaes were no less delightful: the tree is but low, yet spreads gracefully; the fruit is not unlike a sossage for shape, but in taste is most pleasant: they ripen though you crop them immaturely; and from dark green turn into a bright yellow: the rind peels off easily; and the fruit being put into the mouth, dissolves and yields an incomparable relish.*

Lionel Wafer in *A New Voyage and Description of the Isthmus of America* (1699) was already noting the differences between the banana and the plantain:

The Bonano's also grows on the Isthmus very plentifully. They are a sort of Plantains. The fruit is short and thick, sweet and mealy. This eats best raw, and the Plantain boil'd.

The bananas of Brazil were much admired in *A True and Faithful Account of What was Observed in Ten Years Travells into the Principal Places of Europe, Asia, Africa and America* (1665) by R. F. Esq:

For Fruit Trees, besides wild Limons, which grow every wher in great abundance, the Bonano deservedly claims the first place, it being a Tree that from the root grows yearly up to the heighth of an ordinary Plum or Cherry tree, and much about that bulk; tis all green, the body being noth-ing but a collection of the leaves, which spred out towards the Top, and fall like plumes of Feathers, each leaf being some 6 foot in length, and 2 in bredth, on top of which, the fruit grows some 40 together in a bunch, in husks like Beans, all yellow when they are ripe, the fruit of colour and tast much like our Apricock, but much more firm and more delicious.

A Voyage to East-India: wherein some things are taken notice of... by Edward Terry (1655) favours the plantain over English fruit:

They have to these another Fruit we English there call a Planten, of which many of them grow in clusters together; long they are in shape, made unto slender Cucumbers, and very yellow when they are Ripe, and then taste like unto a Norwich Pear, but much better.

A Short Journey in the West Indies in which are interspersed Curious Anecdotes and Characters (1790) indicates what a versatile fruit the plantain is:

The plaintain is a most valuable vegetable, and the grand resource for the poor negroes. It is enclosed in a very thick skin, and used before it is ripe, when it is mealy and very wholesome; in which state it is called bread kind, and often introduced at the best tables. When ripe they are made into fritters or fried. Plantains are from seven inches to upwards of a foot long, and not quite so thick as a man's wrist; they grow in bunches, from fifteen to sixty and more together.

Some Years Travels into Africa & Asia by Sir Thomas Herbert (1677, 4th ed.) warns of a side-effect caused by eating too many plantains:

The Plantain (for tast and odour second to none) ... they hang in clusters like beans upon a branch or stalk, their shape is long and round, not unlike a sausage; if they peel off the rind, the fruit appears of a gold yellow and is relisht like a Windsor pear, so delicious that it melts in ones Mouth leaving a delightful gust, 'tis good for urine but bad for fluxes (meeting with crude stomachs) and if too liberally eaten disposes to dysenteries.

Avocado

Avocados are native to Mexico and were cultivated by the Mesoamericans some 5,000 years ago. Spanish and Portuguese conquistadors encountered the fruit in the sixteenth century and helped spread the plant throughout South America.

Irish naturalist Sir Hans Sloane coined the name avocado in 1696 when he first described the fruit in his book on Jamaican plants but avocados did not become a popular dish in the United Kingdom until the 1920s.

A New Voyage Round the World by Captain William Dampier (1699) includes a description of the avocados of Panama:

The avogato pear-tree is as high, and higher than our pear-trees, with a black, but smooth bark, large oval leaves; the fruit of the bigness of a large lemon, of a green colour at first, but yellow when ripe. The pulp is yellowish, and as soft as butter; and after they have been gathered three or four days, the rind will come off with ease. The stone is as big as a good horse-plum. As this fruit is insipid, so it is commonly eaten with sugar and lime juice, being looked upon by the Spaniards as a great provocative, who have therefore planted them in most places of the North Sea, where they inhabit.

This eighteenth-century book *A Short Journey in the West Indies in which are interspersed Curious Anecdotes and Characters* (1790) indicates that the avocado had become known (though perhaps not tasted) in Europe and references a number of delightful ways to sample it:

The avocado, Sir Hans Sloane's[22] famous vegetable marrow, which is commonly called the Alligator Pear, grows upon a large spreading tree. The pear, as it hangs upon the tree, is not unlike in shape to the large winter baking pear, but much larger and of a very different nature. It does not ripen on the tree, but falls, or is taken when full grown and laid by to ripen, which it does in a few days: the rind is thick, some of a green, others of a purple hue – the fruit it covers is a mixture of green and yellow, and of a consistence something like a cold marrow.

It serves either as a vegetable to accompany meats, or as a fruit takes its place in the desert – sometimes it is cut into small slices as you would cut a melon, and eaten with pepper and salt, sometimes cut in two, and mixed in the rind, with wine and sugar.

---

22 Sir Hans Sloane (1660–1753) was a British doctor who over his lifetime built a large collection of samples, books, prints and curios relating to natural history. Sloane bequeathed his extensive 'cabinet of curiosities' to the nation on his death and much of it made up the collection of the newly opened British Museum, and later that of the Natural History Museum.

Watermelon

Watermelons originated in southern Africa and soon spread up the Nile Valley and on to India and China. By 1576 colonists and slavers had introduced the watermelon to the New World.

The cool, refreshing taste of the watermelon was noted by Edward Terry in his *A Voyage to East-India: wherein some things are taken notice of...* (1655):

> *They have many Water-Melons, a very choyce good Fruit, and some of them as big as our ordinary Pompions [pumpkin], and in shape like them; the substance within this Fruit is spongie, but exceeding tender and well-tasted, of a colour within equally mixed with red & white, and within that an excellent cooling and pleasing liquor.*

Likewise *A Short Journey in the West Indies in which are interspersed Curious Anecdotes and Characters* (1790) admires the qualities of the watermelon:

> *Nothing can be more congenial to this climate than the water melon, being full of a juice as thin as water and almost as pure, but it has sweetness which distinguishes it. When one of these has been lying in cool water, or a cellar, a slice of it is extremely refreshing.*

Granadilla

Granadilla are part of the passion fruit family, and they are native to South America. The fruit of the *Passiflora ligularis* plant, the granadilla are about the size of a plum, have smooth orange rind and are full of small black seeds covered in flavoursome pulp. The following description of the fruit comes from *A Short Journey in the West Indies in which are interspersed Curious Anecdotes and Characters* (1790) and shows that gardeners of England were already attempting to cultivate the plant:

The granadilla is an excellent fruit, one of the finest in the country; it is long, round, and hollow, and grows to a size three times as big as an apple: it is gathered before it is quite ripe, and while it is of a light green colour: in its cavity is contained a juice and a number of little seeds that have a remarkable pleasant acid; this is mixed with sugar and eaten with a spoon: the outside coat when sliced and put into a crust, is hardly to be distinguished from apple-pye. This fruit grows on a vine like that of the passion flower.

Since my return to England, I was conversing with Mr. B. on this subject, who told me that in his father's garden, not far from Windsor, the passion-flower vine bore three granadillas, which were esteemed a great curiosity, but nobody knew what they were, till he, who was just returned from Jamaica, knew the fruit and informed them, on which they were eaten. The vine had never borne before, and died the year after without bearing again.

Unlike many of the other exotic fruits contained in this book the granadilla has not really caught on in Britain (perhaps kept in the metaphoric shade by its more tasty relative, the passion fruit).

Guava

Guava are native to South America and were encountered by Captain William Dampier in Mexico. He wrote of his experience in *A New Voyage Round the World* (1699):

The shrub that bears the guava-fruit has long and small boughs, a white and smooth bark, and leaves like the hazel. The fruit resembles a pear, with a thin rind, and many hard seeds. It may be eaten while green, a thing seldom observed in fruits either in the East or West Indies. It is yellow, soft, and well-tasted. After it is ripe, it may be baked like pears, and will coddle[23] like apples. There are different sorts, distinguished

---

23 Coddling an apple meant to cook it slowly in water.

*by their shape, taste, and colour, some being red, others yellow, in the
inside. Before it is ripe, it is astringent, but afterwards loosening.*

Bread fruit

Breadfruit[24] is native to the Pacific where it was much prized by the
Polynesians, who introduced it to the islands they colonised. This
description from *The Voyages of Pedro Fernandez de Quiros 1595 to
1606* is said to be the earliest recorded European description of the
breadfruit from the Marquesas Islands:

> *The trees which have been mentioned as being in the open space before
> the village yield a fruit which reaches to the size of a boy's head. Its colour,
> when it is ripe, is a clear green, and when unripe it is very green. The
> rind has crossed scales like a pineapple, its shape not quite round, being
> rather more narrow at the end than near the stem. From the stem grows
> a leaf-stalk reaching to the middle of the fruit, with a covering sheath. It
> has no core nor pips, nor anything uneatable except the skin, and that is
> thin. All the rest is a mass of pulp when ripe, not so much when green.
> They feed much upon it in all sorts of ways, and it is so wholesome that
> they call it white food. It is a good fruit and of much substance.*

---

24 When English naturalist Sir Joseph Banks was stationed in Tahiti in 1769 during
his expedition with Captain Cook on the *Endeavour*, he was very struck by the
breadfruit and thought it was such an admirable and useful foodstuff it should be
utilised further. Hearing of his reports, authorities back in Britain thought breadfruit sounded like the ideal high-energy food for the slaves working on plantations
in the Caribbean. In 1787, Captain William Bligh was engaged to sail his ship HMS
Bounty to Tahiti in order to transport large numbers of breadfruit trees to the Caribbean. Unfortunately during the voyage the famous mutiny occurred and Captain
Bligh was expelled from his ship and the trees aboard were lost. Bligh gamely
returned to Tahiti and repeated the endeavour (with 2,126 breadfruit plants aboard),
eventually after an arduous voyage delivering the 678 surviving breadfruit trees to
Jamaica in 1793. Sadly for Bligh all this effort went rather to waste as apparently the
slaves did not care for breadfruit and refused to eat it.

Captain William Dampier in *A New Voyage Round the World* (1699) recorded his impressions of the fruit he found in Guam:

The soil is indifferently fruitful, producing rice, pine-apples, water-melons, musk melons, oranges, limes, cocoanuts, and a certain fruit called the Bread-fruit, growing on a tree as big as our large apple trees, with dark leaves. The fruit is round, and grows on the boughs, like apples, of the bigness of a good penny-loaf. When ripe, it turns yellow, soft and sweet; but the natives take it green, and bake it in an oven, till the rind is black. This they scrape off, and eat the inside, which is soft and white, like the inside of new-baked bread, having neither seed nor stone; but, if it is kept above twenty-four hours, it is harsh.

Durian

The durian has a flavour like no other. It is the Marmite of fruits – people either love it, or hate it. The durian is native to Southeast Asia where it is much appreciated (though not so much on public transport where, due to its very strong aroma, it is frequently banned).

Although European travellers have known of the durian for over 600 years, it has never really caught on in Europe. *A Historical Account of all the Voyages Round the World performed by English Navigators* (1773) quite perfectly sums up the unique flavour of the durian:

The durion takes it name from the word dure, which, in the language of the country, means prickle; and this name is well adapted to the fruit, the shell of which is covered with sharp points shaped like a sugarloaf: its contents are nuts, not much smaller than chesnuts, which are surrounded with a kind of juice resembling cream; and of this the inhab-

itants eat with great avidity: the smell of the fruit is more like that of onions, than any other European vegetable, and its taste is like that of onions, sugar, and cream intermixed.

Cocoa

Drinking chocolate became fashionable amongst Europe's rich in the mid-1600s when Spanish conquistadors brought it back from the New World. The beans were roasted, ground and mixed with water to create a paste which was then dried and made into 'nibs' in order to transport to Europe.

By the eighteenth century chocolate houses had sprung up across Europe; here the nibs were added to sweetened milk and boiled rapidly to create a chocolate drink. It wasn't for another hundred years or so that chocolate became an ingredient used at home in

cakes, biscuits and treats after the development of steam-powered machines made grinding beans quicker and easier, vastly reducing the cost of this commodity.

The History of North and South America (1776) contains the following description of a cacao bean:

The Cocao, or cacao, of which chocolate is made, is a considerable article in the natural history and commerce of New Spain [Mexico, Central America and parts of the Gulf Coast of North America]. It grows upon a tree of middling size; the wood is spongy and porous, the bark smooth, and of a cinnamon colour: the flower grows in bunches between the stalks and the wood, of the form of roses, but small, and without any scent. The fruit is a sort of pod, which contains the cacao, much about the size and shape of a cucumber. Within there is a pulp of a most refreshing acid taste, which fills up the interstices between the nuts before they are ripe; but, when they fully ripen, these nuts are packed up wonderfully close, and in a most regular and elegant order; they have a pretty rough shell, and within this is the oily rich substance of which chocolate is made.

Papaya

Also known as a pawpaw, the papaya originated in Central America, and perhaps due to its high vitamin C content has long been used medicinally. *A Voyage Round the World* by Dr John Francis Gemelli Careri (1700) has this lovely description of a papaya:

The Papayera is a Plant that does not grow above twenty spans high, and the Body of it is under a Span Diameter, but so soft it is easily cut with a knife ... The Papaya it produces, hang like clusters of Grapes about the top of the Trunk, where they Ripen and grow bigger, one after another. In Portuguese Dominions of India they call these the Jesuits Melons, because they taste like Melons and those Fathers like them so well, that they have them every Day at Dinner.

Vanilla

The Totonocan people of the east coast of Mexico were the first to cultivate vanilla and for hundreds of years it was their secret. But by the mid-1400s the Totonocan were conquered by the Aztecs who quickly adopted the vanilla vine, using it to flavour their favourite drink of Xocolatl, or chocolate as we now know it.

In the 1520s Spanish conquistador Hernando Cortes arrived in Mexico and conquered the Aztecs, bringing many of their treasures back to Europe, although the vanilla went largely unnoticed (perhaps due to the rather distracting jaguar, armadillo and Aztec acrobats that Cortes also brought back). Vanilla was simply used as a flavouring in chocolate until 1602 when apothecary to Queen Elizabeth I, Hugh Morgan, tried vanilla as a flavour in its own right.

In the late eighteenth century vanilla plants were taken to the island of Reunion in he Indian Ocean in an effort to set up a plantation. The plants flourished there but the vanilla beans themselves were rarely produced. In 1836 a Belgian botanist Charles Morren realised the problem was a lack of pollination, as back in Mexico a native bee had served that purpose. A local slave, Edmond Albious, invented a method of hand-pollination in 1841 and it was this breakthrough that allowed vanilla to be farmed more productively and trade to flourish.

The following account of the vanilla plant in Mexico comes from *A New Voyage Round the World* by Captain William Dampier (1699) and illustrates the difficulty of extracting the flavour from the plant:

The vinello grows on a small kind of vine, creeping up about the trees. This, at first, bears a yellow flower, which produces a cod of the bigness of the stem of a tobaco-leaf, and about four or five inches long. This cod is green at first, but when ripe becomes yellow: the seeds are black. After they are gathered, they lay them in the sun, which makes them soft, and of a chesnut colour. They squeeze it flat afterwards with the fingers. The

Spaniards, who buy this commodity very cheap of the Indians slake them afterwards with oil. I never heard of any of the vinelloes, except hereabout Caiocha in the bay of Campeachy, and Bocco-torro. Near this last place, I gathered them myself, and endeavoured to cure them, but could not; and as I know other persons, who have lived many years in these parts, and have attempted the same, with no better success, I am apt to believe the Indians have some peculiar way to cure them, that hitherto is unknown to us.

Sugar

Sugar has a long and chequered history – its development as a valuable commodity fuelled the slave trade and contributed to the exploitation of the Caribbean and the New World. Sugar has been known in India for over 5,000 years, it is thought to have been introduced there by Polynesian travellers. From India sugar cane spread to Persia when in 510 BC the emperor Darius conquered India and took 'the reed which gives honey without bees' back to his kingdom.

Arabs took the sugar cane from Persia to North Africa and the Middle East and from thence it came into Portugal and Spain. In 1493, Christopher Columbus, in a game-changing move, took some sugar cane to plant in the Caribbean. The plants flourished and grew faster there than anywhere else. Soon sugar plantations sprang up all over the New World, allowing the mass production of sugar. By 1750 Britain alone ran 120 refining factories and was producing 30,000 tonnes of sugar a year.

Sugar had been known as a very rare and exclusive product in Europe since the Middle Ages but it was not until 1874 when the prime minister, William Gladstone, removed the duty on sugar that ordinary people could afford to enjoy it.

The History of North and South America (1776) contains this description of the sugar cane grown in the West Indies:

The grand staple commodity of the West Indies is sugar; this commodity was not at all known to the Greeks or Romans, though it was made in China in very early times, from whence we had the first knowledge of it; but the Portuguese were the first who cultivated it in America, and brought it into request as one of the materials of a very universal luxury in Europe.

The sugar cane grows to the height of between six and eight feet, full of joints, about four or five inches asunder; the colour of the body of the cane is yellow-ish, and the top where it shoots into leaves, of a vivid green; the coat is pretty hard and within contains a spongy substance, full of a juice, the most lively, elegant, and least cloying

sweet in nature; and which, sucked raw, has proved extremely nutritive and wholesome.

Cashew nut

Native to Brazil, the cashew nut has increased in popularity since India began farming and exporting the nut in the 1920s. What many in Europe do not realise is that the nut grows from a cashew apple, a very popular fruit in its native Brazil. Unfortunately the fruit does not travel well as it begins to ferment within 24 hours of being picked; this has meant that it is mainly only eaten by those who farm the tree.

In the sixteenth century, the Portuguese took cashews from Brazil to India and Mozambique, where the trees flourished. It was not until the nineteenth century that cashews began to be farmed more intensively but because of the caustic oils contained in the outer shell the nuts proved hard to market. In the 1920s Sri Lankan Roch Victoria developed a method to remove the outer shell and international trade took off.

A True and Faithful Account of What was Observed in Ten Years Travells into the Principal Places of Europe, Asia, Africa and America by R. F. Esq (1665) contains this account of the cashews of Brazil:

> *For their Caijus, it is a sort of Tree of the bignes of our ordinary Apple-trees, the leaves like chesnut leaves, and fruit much like the bigger sort of green Figs, fastend to the Tree in lieu of stalk, by certain Chesnuts, which roasted are excellent meat, the fruit eaten whole, melts all away to juice, exceeding cooling and refreshing, excepting certain strings which hang in your teeth, so tough, you cannot swallow them.*

Nutmeg, mace, cloves and cinnamon

Nutmeg, cloves and cinnamon have been known in Europe since the Middle Ages, when Arabs traded them to the Venetians. As with most exotic spices they were the preserve of the very rich due to the difficulty of sourcing and shipping large quantities to Europe. Indeed such was the circuitous route taken by spices, passing through the hands of many traders, by the time they arrived in Europe it was unclear in which country they had originated.

After the Dutch gained control of much of Indonesia in the 1600s they secured a monopoly on the spice trade, which held for over 150 years through the mighty Dutch East India Company. This ensured the spices remained valuable and relatively scarce (indeed the Dutch deliberately limited the harvest of spices to keep the prices sky high).

Nutmeg is native to the Banda Islands of Indonesia and the Dutch held a tight hold on its trade after gaining control of the tiny Indonesian island of Run, one of the few places where nutmeg was

grown at that time. Dutch sailor Christopher Fryke described the nutmeg tree in *A Relation of Two Several Voyages made into the East Indies* (1700):

The Tree on which the Nutmeg grows, is almost like the Pear-tree, but doth not spread so much, and its Leaf is somewhat rounder. The Fruit is much like Peach in bigness and looks of an extraordinary fine taste, and delicate smell when it is ripe: On the outside is thick hard Shell, like the Bark of a Tree, over which the Flower grows. When the Nut begins to be ripe it swells so much, that the first shell bursts open. The Flower is of a fine Red, and very agreeable to look on, especially when the Tree is pretty full of Fruit. Sometimes the Mace comes off of itself and when it sticks to the Fruit, they gather all together; and in the drying of the Nutmeg, the Mace dries and falls off, and changes its lively Red into that brown Yellow, which we find it hath here in Europe.

The British broke the Dutch monopoly on nutmeg and mace in 1817 when they planted nutmeg trees in the British Overseas territories of Grenada, Sri Lanka and Singapore, allowing production to increase significantly.

Cloves are also native to Indonesia (the Moluccas or Spice Islands) where they held a special importance for the locals, who had a custom of planting a clove tree to celebrate the birth of a new baby. In order to keep control of the clove trade, the Dutch wanted to make sure clove trees were only grown in areas under their control and thus had a policy of cutting down or burning cloves trees not in their plantations. This angered the local population who did their best to protect some of the 'rogue' trees. One such tree on the island of Tidore was to prove the Dutch's undoing. In 1770 a Frenchman known, somewhat mysteriously, as Monsieur Poivre stole some clove seeds from a surviving tree and took them to Zanzibar where the trees soon flourished allowing the clove trade to open up. In *A Relation of Two Several Voyages made into the East Indies* (1700) Christopher Fryke described the clove tree:

The Clove-Tree is much like the Laurel-Tree, the Blossom is White at first, then it turns Green, and after that Red. While it is green is smells so fine and sweet, that nothing can be compared to it ... The smell of 'em is so strong, that some people have been suffocated with it when they have been busie with too great quantities of 'em, and in too close a place.

Cinnamon came under Dutch control when they took Ceylon (Sri Lanka) from the Portuguese in 1638 and it remained in their hands until 1784 when the British took over. Christopher Fryke also described the cinnamon trees he encountered in Ceylon:

The great Commodity of this Island is Cinnamon, which is the Bark of a Tree, much of the bigness of an Olive Tree; the Leaves are much like the Laurel, but somewhat smaller; the Flower it bears is white, and the fruit is like the Black Olives of Portugal. The Tree hath two Barks, the Cinnamon is the inner one of them, which is peeled off the Tree, and cut in square pieces; then laid in the Sun to dry, which makes it rowl up together, as we see it in Europe, and changes its colour, which is at first near upon Ash-colour into what we find it of here.

Another Dutchman, Francois Valentijn, recorded his impressions of the cinnamon tree in *Francois Valentijn's Descriptions of Ceylon* (1724):

The most important tree, the island's own, is the cinnamon tree. The Cingalese call it corindo-gas ... This tree has double bark, the outermost, which is not cinnamon and which one first peels with a knife, and the innermost which is the real cinnamon and is peeled with the curved edge of a knife first in a circle and then lengthwise, and laid to dry in the sun where they roll into each other and are curled together as we generally see them.

After the tree is thus peeled, it does not grow any further but new trees grow from the fruits. The wood of this tree gives out no smell except when burnt, being white and soft, almost like fir wood, which the natives use in making houses and in the construction of fine cabinets and tables.

Mangosteen

Mangosteen are native to Indonesia and are now common across Southeast Asia. Perhaps due to the fact that they must ripen on the tree and once picked stay fresh for only a short time, the mangosteen has not become a popular exotic fruit in Britain.

Dutch explorer Christopher Fryke, author of *A Relation of Two Several Voyages made into the East Indies* (1700) would no doubt be surprised that the tasty fruit never caught on:

But of all the fruits that the East-Indies produce ... I think it will not be amiss to give you a description ... of the chiefest of them. That which deserves the first place amongst them, is the fruit which they call the Manges Tanges; of the bigness of a common Apple; the shell is of a dark brown colour, in which are contained four Kernels, of a flesh colour, sticking to each other, which melt like Butter upon the Tongue, and of so fine and refreshing a taste, that I have never met with any fruit comparable to it, in any other part of the World.

A Historical Account of all the Voyages Round the World performed by English Navigators (1773) was equally impressed:

The mangostan is of a dark red colour, and not larger than a small apple; to the bottom of this fruit adhere several little leaves of the blossom, while on its top are a number of triangles combined in a circle: it contains several kernals ranged in a circular form, within which is the pulp, a fruit of most exquisite taste: it is equally nutritious and agreeable, and is constantly given to persons who are troubled with inflammatory or putrid fevers.

Coffee

Coffee originates from Ethiopia and was a relatively modern discovery, its use first mentioned in the fifteenth century. The stimulating effects of coffee ensured its popularity and it was initially used by Sufi monks in Yemen to stay awake for night-time prayer.

By the early fifteenth century coffee had spread to Mecca, a major meeting place for the Muslim world, allowing the bean to disperse across the Middle East. Travellers soon brought coffee to Europe and legend has it that in the early 1600s Pope Clement VIII was asked to ban coffee due to suspicions that it was the devil's drink (it being the favourite drink of the infidel Ottoman Empire), but on tasting the brew Pope Clement gave it his blessing.

Coffee houses soon sprang up all over Europe as people rushed to try the new drink. In England the first coffee houses opened in the mid-seventeenth century and they soon became meeting places and centres of debate which typify the spirit of the Age of Enlightenment.

William Biddulph wrote of his first experience of coffee in Turkey in *The Travels of Four Englishmen and a Preacher into Africa, Asia, Troy, Bythinia, Thracia, and to the Blacke Sea* (1612):

Their most common drink is Coffa, which is a black kind of drink made of a kind of paste like Pease, called Coaua; which being ground in the mill, and boiled in water, they drinke it as hot as they can suffer it; which they find to agree very well with them against their crudities and feeding on hearbes and raw meats.

Italian explorer Pietro della Valle (1586–1652) gives a thorough description of Turkish coffee in *Travels in Persia* (published in English in 1658):

The Turks have a Drink of a black Colour, which during the summer is very cooling, whereas in the Winter it mightily heats and warms the Body ... This Drink, as I remember is made with the grain or Fruit of a certain Tree, which grows in Arabia towards Mecca, and the fruit it produces is called Cahue, whence this drink derives its Name, 'tis of an oval shape, of the same bigness as a middle-sized Olive, and to make this composition they take sometimes no more than the skin, which is tender, sometimes only the Kernel, which is like to beans; and they are of an opinion, that of these two juices, the one heats and t'other cools, but I cannot well call to mind whether the refreshing is that of the skin or the other.

The way to make the Drink thereof, is thus: They burn the skin or Kernel of this fruit as it best pleases their fancy or palate, and they beat it to a powder very fine, of a blackish colour, which is not very pleasant to the eye-sight ... When they would drink thereof they boyl it in Water in certain pots made on purpose ... Afterwards they pour out this Liquor to be drunk as hot as the Mouth and Throat can endure it, not suffering themselves to swallow it but by little and little and at several times, because of its actual heat; and after it has taken the taste and colour of this powder, whereof the thick sinks down and remains at the bottom of the Pot, to make use of it more deliciously, they mingle with this powder of Cahue, much Sugar, Cinnamon and Cloves well beaten, which gives it an exquisite taste and makes it much more nourishing.

The Manner of Making of Coffee, Tea and Chocolate as it is used in most parts of Europe, Asia, Africa and America (1685) reflects the new-found enthusiasm for this new drink across Europe:

Although the use and eating of Beans, were heretofore forbidden by Pythagoras, because that their flowers being spotted with a black Colour, did present a melancholy shape, and the Souls of the dead that did dwell therein: And though there be others that reject them, affirming that the use of them dulls the senses, and causes troublesome Dreams: Yet because they serve us in the Nature of Victuals and Physick, I shall not think my time and labour mis imployed, if I communicate to the publick, something on this Subject of Beans.

I will speak for the present of a certain Bean of Arabia called Bon, where of they make a Drink termed Coffee, which was heretofore in use amongst Arabians and Egyptians and which is now a dayes in very great request amongst the English, French, and Germanes.

Coffee is a Berry which only grows in the desert of Arabia, from whence it is transported into all the Dominions of the Grand Seigniour, which being drunk dries up all the cold and moist humours, disperses the wind, fortifies the Liver, eases the dropsie by its purifying quality, 'tis a Sovereign medicine against the itch, and corruptions of the blood, refreshes the heart, and the vital beating thereof.

Such was the popularity of coffee by the end of the seventeenth century that there were thousands of coffee houses in all the major cities of Europe and demand was growing. The Arabs had tried to keep a monopoly on the coffee trade but the wily Dutch managed to acquire some seedlings which they successfully transported to Batavia (Java, Indonesia) and established plantations.

In 1714 the Dutch presented the French king, Louis XIV, with some coffee seedlings which he then planted in the Royal Botanical Gardens in Paris. Gabriel de Clieu, a young naval officer, took some cuttings of the plant in 1723 and in spite of a long and difficult voyage including attacks by pirates, he managed to safely transport the coffee plants to Martinique where they flourished. Within the next fifty years from those few seedlings nearly 18 million coffee plants were planted and from that stock the coffee tree spread into the Caribbean and the New World.

Today one of the largest producers of coffee is Brazil, and there is a rather nice story of how the bean spread to this part of the world. In 1727 Francisco de Mello Palheta was sent to French Guiana in order to try and negotiate some coffee seedlings for Brazil. The French were not keen to share their bounty and refused. The story goes that the governor's wife was so taken with the rather dashing de Mello Palheta that she presented him with a large bouquet of flowers hidden within which were enough coffee seeds to start a plantation.

PEOPLE, PLACES & CUSTOMS

Australia – aborigines

In 1699 privateer and mapmaker Captain William Dampier was the first Briton to set foot on Australian soil. His *A Voyage to New Holland, &c. in the Year 1699* (1703) contains this rather typical account of clumsy European attempts to make contact with natives:

While we were at work [digging for water], there came nine or ten of the natives, to a small hill a little way from us, and stood there menacing and threatening, and making a great noise. At last one of them came towards us, and the rest followed at a great distance. I went out to meet him, and came within fifty yards of him, making to him all the signs of peace and friendship I could; but then he ran away, neither would any of them stay for us to come nigh them, though we tried three or four times. At last I took two men with me, and went in the afternoon along the sea-side, on purpose to catch one of them if I could, of whom I might learn where they got their fresh water. There were ten or twelve of the natives a little way off, who seeing us three going away from the rest of our men, followed us ... We knew by what rencounter we had with them in the morning we could easily out-run them; so a nimble young man that was with me, seeing some of them there, ran towards them, and they, for some time, ran away before him, but he soon overtaking them, they faced about, and fought him. He has a cutlass, and they had wooden lances, with which, being many of them, they were too hard for him. When he first ran towards them, I chased two more, that were by

the shore; but, fearing how it might be with my young man, I turned
back quickly, and went up to the top of a sandy hill, whence I saw him
near me, and closely engaged with them. Upon seeing me, one of them
threw a lance, which narrowly missed me. I discharged my gun to scare
them; but avoided shooting any of them, till finding my young man in
great danger, and myself in some, and that though the gun had a little
frightened them at first, they had soon learnt to despise it, tossing up
their hands, and crying, pooh, pooh, pooh, and coming on a-fresh with
a great noise, I thought it time I charge a-fresh, and shoot one of them,
which I did. The rest, seeing him fall, made a stand; and my young man
took the opportunity to disengage himself, and come off to me. They took
up their wounded companion; and my young man, who had been struck
through the cheek by one of their lances was afraid it was poisoned, But
I did not think it likely.

Australia was formally colonised by the British in 1788. George Barrington, an inveterate pickpocket, was transported to Australia in 1790. During the voyage he foiled a plot to overthrow the ship's Captain and this and subsequent good behaviour meant that he was the first convict to receive a warrant of emancipation. In a rather startling change of fortunes Barrington went on to become High Constable of Parramatta.[25] In *A Voyage to New South Wales* (1796) Barrington described the aborigines he encountered:

I had many opportunities of getting acquainted with several of the
natives; and, as I seldom saw them without giving them some trifle or

---

25 Barrington recounted how the British settlement in New South Wales grew as the convicts completed their sentences: 'Having a good deal of time on my hands, my attendance and inspection being generally finished in the forenoon, I frequently visited the farms of the settlers: these in general were convicts whose term of transportation had expired, and had had lands granted them, in the following proportions: thirty acres to every single man; fifty to the married ones; and ten more for every child: they received provisions and clothing from the public stores for the first eighteen months: the necessary tools and implements of husbandry, with seeds and grain to sow the ground the first year: two young sow pigs were also given to each settler, and a pair or two of fowls.'

other, soon became a great favourite with them, and mostly had one or other of them with me in my rambles. The men in general are from five feet six to five feet nine inches high; are rather slender, but straight and well made. The women are not quite so tall, rather lustier, but are mostly well made. Their colour is brownish black, of a coffee cast, but many of the women are almost as light as a mulatto: now and then you may meet with some of both sexes with pretty tolerable features, but broad noses, wide mouths, and thick lips, are most generally met with; their countenances are not the prepossessing, and what renders them still less so, is, they are abominably filthy. They know no such ceremony as washing themselves; their skin is mostly smeared with the fat of such animals as they kill, and afterwards covered with every sort of dirt; sand from the beach, and ashes from their fires, all adhere to their filthy skin, which never comes off except when accident, or the want of food obliges them to go into the water. Some of the men wear a piece of wood, or bone thrust through the septum of the nose, which, by raising the opposite sides of the nose, dilates the nostril, and spreads the lower part very much.

They have, in general, good teeth; their hair is short, strong, and curly; and they having no method of combing or cleaning it, it is always filthy and matted: the men's beards are short and curly like the hair of their heads. They all go entirely naked, men, women, and children, and seem to have no fixed place of residence, but lay down wherever night overtakes them. Cavities in the rocks on the sea shore, are places they usually seek to shelter themselves from the wind and rain; and they mostly

143

make a good fire before they go to sleep, by which means the rock round them becomes heated, and retains its warmth a considerable time, like an oven; and spreading a little dried grass they lie down and huddle together.

The men are generally armed with a lance, and a short stick which they use in throwing it; this stick is about a yard long, flat on one side, and a notch in one end, the other is furnished with a flat shell fixed into a split in the stick, made fast with a strong gum, which, when dry, is as hard as flint: on the flat side of the stick they place the lance, the butt end of which rests against the notch in the throwing stick; poising the lance thus fixed in one hand, binding it with the fore finger and thumb to prevent its slipping off; keeping fast hold of the throwing stick, they hurl the lance with considerable force, and tolerably true, to the distance of seventy or eighty yards.

When they are upon any hostile expedition, they paint their faces and bodies with red and white streaks, as if they intended to strike terror by their death-like appearance.

In *Voyage to Australia* by Sinclair Thomson Duncan (1884) the author displays rather typically Victorian opinions on the aborigines:

The aborigines of Australia are a peculiar looking class of people, understood to be the lowest grade of the human race, of a dark copper colour, have thick lips, large mouth, flat nose, sunken in eyes, long black hair, little or no calf to their legs, and walk about almost naked. ... They are savages, have been known to eat human flesh, and it is with great difficulty they can be trained to lead anything like a civilised life.

Pacific & Asia – chewing betel nut

Betel nuts come from the areca palm which is native to the Pacific, Asia and east Africa. It is traditionally chewed wrapped in betel leaves with slaked lime and is a mild stimulant (some have described its effects as similar to drinking a cup of strong coffee).

Betel nuts have differing traditional uses depending on the country – in some places their use is mainly medicinal, in other countries, such as Malaysia, offering betel is a sign of hospitality. The betel nut is still widely used across Asia and the practice is most commonly associated with red-stained teeth and frequent spitting.

Spanish explorer Alvaro Mendaña reached the Solomon Islands in 1567 and it is thought he was the first European to describe the custom of chewing betel nuts in *The Narrative of Mendaña* (1567):

There are Indians of different complexions in this island; some are the same colour as those of Peru, others are black, and a few quite fair, these being either they who rarely leave their houses, or young boys. They all curl or dye their hair, and some dye it a light colour; some are naturally fair. The women are better looking than those of Peru, but they disfigure

themselves greatly blackening their teeth ... Their tongue and lips are
very red, for they colour them with a herb which they eat; it has a broad
leaf, and burns like pepper; they chew this herb with lime which they
make from white lucianos, which is a stone formed in the sea like coral;
and having a piece of lime in their mouths, it makes a red juice, and this
is why their tongues and lips are always so red; they also smear their
faces with this juice for ornament. Although they chew this herb, they do
not get this red juice unless they mix it with said lime.

A Voyage to East-India: wherein some things are taken notice of... by
Edward Terry (1655) includes this description of betel nut chewing
in India:

There is yet another help for those that forbear Wine, by an herb they
have, called Beetle or Paune, in shape somewhat like a Nutmeg (but not
in tast like that) and a very little pure white-lime amongst the leaves,
and when they have sucked down the juice, put forth the rest. It hath
(as they say and I believe very much of it) many rare qualities, for it
preserves the Teeth, strengthens the Stomack, comforts the Brain, and
it cures and prevents a tainted Breath. This I am sure of, that such is
the pleasing smell of this Beetle, being chewed in a close room, that the
breath of him so chewing it fills it with a very pleasing savour.

The Travels of Peter Mundy in Europe and Asia 1608–1667 (1667) also
recounted betel nut chewing in India:

Wee also sawe some feilds of Paan, which is a kinde of leafe much used
to bee eaten in this Countrie, thus: First they take a kinde of Nutt called
Saparoz, and commonly with use Bettlenutt, which, broken to peeces, they
infold in one of said leaves, and soe put it into their mouthes. Then take
they of the said leaves, and puttinge a little slaked lyme on them, they
also put into their mouthes, and after them other, untill their mouthes
are reasonably filled, which they goe champinge, swalloweing downe the
Juice till it be drie; then they spitt it out. It is accompted a grace to eat it up
and downe the streets and used by great men. There is no vesitt, banquett,

etts. without it, with which they passe away the tyme, as with Tobaccoe in England: but this is very wholsome, sweete in smell, and stronge in Taste. To Strangers it is most comonly given att partinge, soe that when they send for Paane, it is a signe of dispeedinge, or that it is tyme to be gon.

Madagascar – the people

Europeans first learned of Madagascar in 1500 when it was spotted by Diogo Dias, a Portuguese sailor. By the end of the seventeenth century the French began setting up trading posts on the coast of the island.

British merchant trader Peter Mundy recorded his impressions of Madagascar in *The Travels of Peter Mundy in Europe and Asia 1608–1667* (1667):

> *St Lawrence, antiently called Madagascar, is held to bee one of the greatest Islands that are yett discovered. The Land about Augustine Bay is faire, round and pleasant to see to, aboundinge with woods and a large freshwater river, both which are replenished with foule and fish of severall sorts, differinge from those in our parts. The people black, well proportioned, strong lym'd, active, healthie, tractable and sociable with us: the haire of their heads made into little plates, hanging round about, and somme have part thereof bound upright on the Crowne of their heads, which they annoint with butter, oyle, or grease, which of them come first to hand. There weapons, Darts: generally goeinge naked, except haveing a Cloth to cover their Privities ... We bartered with them Cornelion[26] beades for Bullocks, of which heere are the fairest that I have els where seene ... The Cornelion beades aforementioned are by them esteemed above any other Treasure, for, offer them peeces of gold or gold ringes with precious stones in them, they refuse all for the Bead, the other not knowne or accompted of amongst them. Soe that for 7 or 8 of those Beades, scarse worth 7d. a peece in India, we should have a Bullock worth 3 or 4 li. in England.*

---

26 Carnelian is an orange/red semi-precious stone. It was valued by the ancient Egyptians, Greeks and Romans, and due to its hardness was often used in signet rings.

India – attitude towards animals

It was not just the exotic animals, plants and foods that inspired the awe of travellers. At times it was the cultural differences which really struck the explorers. Here Edward Terry in *A Voyage to East-India: wherein some things are taken notice of...* (1655) marvels at the Indian attitude towards animals:

> For they will not (if they can help it by any means) take, but on the contrary do what they can to preserve the lives of all inferior Creatures, whence (as before I told you) they give large money to preserve the lives of their Kine (a reason for this you shall have afterward) and I have often observed, that when our English boyes there have out of wantonesse been killing of Flies (there swarming in abundance) they would be very much troubled at it, and if they could not perswade them to suffer those poor Creatures to live, they would give them money, or something else to forbear that (as they conceived) cruelty.
>
> As for themselves (I mean a very great number of them) they will not deprive the most uselesse, and most offensive Creatures of life, not Snakes, and other venomous things that may kill them, saying, that it is their nature to do hurts, and they cannot help it, but as for themselves they further say, that God hath given them reason to shun those Creatures, but not liberty to destroy them.

North America – Native American people

The arrival of Europeans in America has come under a great deal of scrutiny in recent years, with new evidence that the Vikings may have landed in America hundreds of years before Christopher Columbus did in 1492. Whatever the truth, Native Americans had inhabited the lands for over twelve thousand years.

As Europeans began to explore and colonise North America from the 1600s they inevitably encountered the many Native American tribes.

The History of North and South America (1776) contains the following description of the Native Americans. It is interesting to note the reflection on the behaviour of the contemporary Europeans:

The Americans are tall, and strait in their limbs beyond the propor-
tions of most nations; their bodies are strong; but of a species of strength
rather fitted to endure much hardship, than to continue long at any
servile work, by which they are quickly consumed. Their bodies and
heads are flattish, the effect of art; their features are regular, but their
countenances fierce; their hair long, black, lank, and very strong, but

*without beards. The colour of their skin is a reddish brown, admired
amongst them, and improved by the constant use of bear's fat and paint.*

*The Indians are grave even to sadness in their deportment upon any
serious occasion: observant of those in company; respectful to the old; of
a temper cool and deliberate: by which they are never in haste to speak
before they have thought well upon the matter, and are sure the person
who spoke before them has finished all he had to say. They have therefore
the greatest contempt for the vivacity of the Europeans, who interrupt
each other, and frequently speak all together. Nothing is more edifying
than their behaviour in their public councils and assemblies. Every
man there is heard in his turn, according as his years, his wisdom, or
his services to his country have ranked him. Not a word, not a whisper,
Not a murmur, is heard from the rest while he speaks.*

Australia – the boomerang

Boomerangs or throwing sticks have become indelibly linked with
Australia. It is thought that this is partly due to the fact that aborigines never developed a bow and arrow for hunting and so boomerangs were advanced instead.

Archaeological evidence points to the existence of non-re-
turning boomerangs across Stone Age Europe, and returning
boomerangs have been found in ancient Egypt and amongst some
Native American tribes. *Kangaroo and Kauri* by J. K. Arthur (1894)
contains this description of the boomerangs the author observed in
Australia:

*The Australian aboriginals, even the youngsters, are very skilful in
the precision with which they throw missiles or projectiles of various
kinds. These people have been known to take up stones with their feet
and throw them with almost as accurate an aim as ordinary men will
have with their hands. With a piece of slightly curved thick bark, hastily
torn from a tree, they are able to hit another person though he stands
behind the shelter of another tree. The instrument so used is an extem-*

porized "boomerang" or "kylie". The boomerangs used in England have a sharper curve than the Australian, which is made of a curved piece of wood, flat on one side and slightly rounded on the other. It was much used by the natives, who could throw it very dexterously. It should be held horizontally in throwing, and cast by bringing the arm backwards. After making a variety of curves, it will come back to the person who threw it. If skilfully thrown, it may be made to go in almost any direction the thrower pleases.

India – modes of dress

Pietro Della Valle gives an interesting glimpse of the modes of dress in India in the seventeenth century in *Travels in Persia* (1658):

Upon this occasion I must not forget, that amongst the Indian Men, both Mahometans and Pagans, agreeably to what Strabo testifies, they did of old wear onely white linnen, more or less fine according to the quality of the persons, and the convenience they have of spending: which linnen is altogether of Bumbast or Cotton, (there being no Flax in India) and for the most part very fine in comparison of those of our Countries. The garment which they put next to their skin, serves both for Coat and Shirt from the girdle upwards, being adorn'd upon the breast, and hanging down in many folds to the middle of the Leg. Under this cassack from the

girdle downwards, they wear a pair of long Drawers of the same Cloth,
which cover not only their Thighs, but legs also to the Feet; and 'tis a
piece of gallantry to have it wrinkled in many folds, upon the legs. The
naked Feet are no otherwise confin'd but to a slipper; and that easie to
be pull'd off without the help of the Hand; this mode being convenient,
in regard the heat of the Country, and the frequent use of standing or
walking upon Tapistry in their Chambers.

Papua New Guinea – first impressions

First spotted by Spanish explorers in the sixteenth century, Papua
New Guinea remained largely unexplored by Europeans until the
nineteenth century when some settlements were established.

Captain Thomas Forrest, an English navigator, worked for the
British East India Company and in 1774 undertook to explore New
Guinea. His account *A Voyage to New Guinea* (1779) contains this
description of the people he there encountered:

Two Papua men, came on board, after having conversed a good deal
with our linguists at a distance: satisfied we were friends, they hastened
ashore, to tell, I suppose, the news. Soon after, many Papua Coffres came
on board, and were quite easy and familiar: all of them wore their hair
brushed out so much round their heads, that its circumference measured
about three foot, and where least, two and a half. In this they stuck their
comb, consisting of four or five long diverging teeth, which they now and
then combed their frizzling locks, in a direction perpendicular from the
head, as with a design to make it more bulky. They sometimes adorned
their hair with feathers.

Forrest went on to reveal some of the food he tasted there:

The Papua people in their boats, continued to bring us abundance of
excellent fish; also turtle, which my Mahometans [Muslims] would not
eat; but they ate the eggs. The natives had a way of stuffing the guts of

the turtle, with the yolks of its eggs. So filled, they rolled it up in a spiral form, and roasted it, or rather dried it over a slow fire; it proved then a long sausage.

The sad story of an English sailor

The attitudes and behaviour of some of the European sailors towards the people they encountered on their travels can sometimes seem unbelievable to modern eyes. However there is evidence that some contemporary travellers were equally offended by the conduct of their fellow Europeans.

French traveller John Mocquet recounted this tragic tale[27] in his 1617 book. This is the English version published some years later in *Travels and Voyages into Africa, Asia and America, the East and West-Indies; Syria, Jerusalem and the Holy-Land* (1696):

Our Trumpeter shewed me their Pilot, and told me, that he some years before being in an English Vessel, as they were upon the Coasts of the West Indies, towards St. John de Love, (the first place of the Indies to go to Mexico, where the Spaniards are, then their Sworn Enemies) a great Storm overtook them, which cast them upon the Coast, where they were all lost, except this Pilot, who saved himself by Swimming to Land, carrying with him a little Sea-Compass, and went thus wandring about to return by Land to the Newfound Countries: Upon that, he had found an Indian-Woman, of whom he was Enamoured, making her fine Promises by Signs, that he would Marry her; which she believed, and conducted him through these Desarts; where she shewed him the Fruit and Roots good to Eat, and served him for an Interpreter amongst the Indians, which he found, she telling them that it was her Husband. After having been thus 2 or 3 years continually wandering about, and that for above 800 Leagues, without any other Comfort but this Woman: At last they arrived at Newfoundland, guiding himself by his Compass: They had a child together; and found there an English ship a Fishing: He was very glad to see himself escaped from so many Dangers, and gave these English an account of all his Adventures: They took him on Board their Vessel to make him good chear; but being ashamed to take along with him this Indian-Woman thus Naked, he left her on Land, without regarding her any more: But she seeing herself thus forsaken by him, whom she had so dearly Loved, and for whose sake she had abandoned her Country and Friends, and had so well guided and accompanied him through such places where he would, without her, have been dead a thousand times. After having made some Lamentation, full

---

27 This story is said to have inspired first Richard Ligon (writing in prison in 1657) and then Richard Steele (writing in *The Spectator* in 1711) to create the legend of Yarico and Inkle, which was later performed as an opera.

of Rage and Anger, she took her Child, and tearing it into two pieces, she cast the one half towards him into the Sea, as if she would say, that belonged to him, and this was his part of it; and the other she carried away with her, returning back to the Mercy of Fortune, and full of Mourning and Discontent.

The Seamen who took this Pilot into their Boat, seeing this horrible and cruel spectacle, asked him, why he had left this Woman; but he pretended she was a Savage, and that he did not now heed her; which was an extream Ingratitude and Wickedness in him: Hearing this, I could not look upon him, but always with Horrour and great Detestation.

India – smoking tobacco

Tobacco was traditionally smoked by Native Americans, usually as part of a religious ceremony. Christopher Columbus was the first European to encounter tobacco in the New World in 1492. By the late 1520s the Spanish were importing tobacco to Europe and it became very popular – many believed it had medicinal properties – and from here its use spread around the world.

A Voyage to East-India: wherein some things are taken notice of... by Edward Terry (1655) has the following observations on tobacco smoking in India:

They sow Tobacco in abundance, and they take it too very much, but after a strange way much different from us; for first, they have little Earthen Pots, shaped like our small flower-pots, having a narrow neck, and an open round top, out of the belly of which comes a small spout, to the lower part of which spout they fill the Pot with water, then putting their Tobacco loose in the top, and a burning coal upon it, they having first fastened a very small strait hollow Cane or Reed (not bigger than a small Arrow) within that spout, a yard or ell long, the Pot standing on the ground, draw that smoak into their mouths, which first falls upon the Superficies of the water, and much discolours it. And this way of taking their Tobacco, they believe, makes it much more cool and wholsome. The

Tobacco which grows there is doubtless in the Plant as good as in any other place in the world, but they know not how to cure and order it, like those in the West-Indies, to make it so rich and strong.

The Philippines – the people

Claimed for the Spanish Empire in 1521 by Ferdinand Magellan, the Philippines became an important trading hub. *The Voyages of Pedro Fernandez de Quiros 1595 to 1606* contains the Portuguese navigator's impressions of the inhabitants:

The natives here are of a brown colour, not very tall, and their bodies tattooed. They have no beards, nor any sign of them. Their hair is black and long. Their loins are covered with cloth, and in the villages they wore a tunic of the same material, with no colour, and reaching down to their calves. They have large gold earrings, ivory armlets, and similar ornaments on their legs, of gilded bronze, which deceived some of our people. These natives are so selfish that without silver or something they want in exchange, they will give nothing.

The natives came morning and evening, bringing and bartering their produce, so that in fourteen days provisions were collected for the rest of the voyage.

Japan – diving for fish

John Saris was the captain of the first British ship to sail to Japan. Sent to negotiate trade with the Japanese, Saris befriended the Shogun Tokugawa Hidetada and collected many Japanese arte-facts.[28] His account *The Voyage of John Saris to Japan* (1613) includes

---

28 You can still see one of the beautiful Japanese suits of armour John Saris brought back to England at the Tower of London. Unfortunately not all of his souvenirs were appreciated – his collection of erotic Japanese paintings (shunga) was confiscated and destroyed by the East India Company.

this description of the traditional Japanese skill of free diving for fish:

> *All alongst the Coast, and so up to Ozaca [Osaka], we found women divers, that lived with their houshold and family in boats upon the water, as in Holland they do the like. These women would catch fish by diving, which by net and lines they missed, and that in eight fathome depth: their eyes by continuall diving doe grow as red as blood, whereby you may know a diving woman from all other women.*

Tahiti – the people

An *Abridgement of Captain Cook's First and Second Voyages* (1788) includes the following impression of the people of Otaheite [Tahiti]:

> *With regard to the people, they are in general rather of a larger make than Europeans. The males are tall, robust and finely shaped. The females of the superior class are likewise generally above our common size; but those of the lower rank are rather below it; and some of them are remarkably little.*
>
> *Their natural complexion is a fine clear olive, or what we call brunette; their skin is delicately smooth and agreeably soft. The shape of their faces is in general handsome, and their eyes are full of sensibility and expression; their teeth are likewise remarkably white and regular, and their breath intirely free from any disagreeable smell.*

The account of Portuguese navigator Pedro Fernandez de Quiros in *The Voyages of Pedro Fernandez de Quiros 1595 to 1606* includes this lovely scene of the sailors meeting with a native of the Chain Islands, near Tahiti:

> *When they went down to embark they saw a shape which appeared to be that of a man, coming towards them at a short distance. They went to see what it was, and found that it was an old woman, who appeared to be*

a hundred years of age: a tall and large woman, with fine and long black hairs and only four or five grey ones, her colour brown, face and body wrinkled, teeth few and decayed, and with other faults caused by a long life. She came along, waving with soft palm leaves. She carried some cuttle-fish dried in the sun, in a basket, and a knife made from a mother-of-pearl shell, also a skein of thread. A little speckled dog accompanied her, which ran away.

With this good capture the boat returned to the Captain, to show her to him, who was highly delighted at seeing a human creature. He seated her on a box, and gave her meat and soup from a pot, which she ate without scruple; but she could not manage the hard biscuit. She showed that she knew well how to drink wine. A mirror was put into her hand, and she looked at the back, then at the front, and when she saw her face she was much pleased. All noticed her good manners, and concluded that, when young, she was not bad-looking. She looked at all the men with attention, but she displayed the greatest pleasure in looking at the boys. She looked at the goats as if she had seen them before. There was a gold ring with an emerald on one of her fingers. She was asked for it, but replied by signs that she could not give it without cutting off her finger,

and she seemed very sorry for this. She was offered one of brass which she did not care for. Having given her things to dress herself with and take away, we saw four canoes coming from the village under sail, out of a lake which the island has at its centre, and they anchored near a palm grove. The Captain presently ordered the old woman to be landed to reassure the natives. They no sooner recognised her than they came to see her and looked at her as if she had been long absent. They came to our people with the confidence of friends.

China – an agreeable prospect

Known in Europe since Medieval times, China still held great mystery to most ordinary Europeans. The writings of Marco Polo in 1300 provided the first account of China but it wasn't until the sixteenth century that trading posts were established.

Voyage from New South Wales to Canton in the year 1788 by Thomas Gilbert (1789) contains this description of China:

As you sail up the river of Canton, the country exhibits an agreeable prospect. For the first part, the ground on each side is level, and laid out in rice-fields; but, as you advance, it rises gradually into hills, the sides of which are cut into terraces, and planted with sugar-canes, yams, plan- tains, and the cotton-tree. The view is enlivened by many lofty pagodas, and a number of considerable towns within the reach of the eye.

India – the flowers

A Voyage to East-India: wherein some things are taken notice of... by Edward Terry (1655) includes this observation on the flowers of India:

For their Flowers, they are for the generality like unto painted Weeds, which, though their colour be excellent, they rather delight the eye than affect the smell; for not many of them, except Roses, and some few kinds more, are any whit fragrant: Amongst them that are, there is one white Flower, like to Spanish Jessamin (if it not be the same) which is exceedingly well sented, of which they make the most excellent pure sweet Oyl, with which they annoyt their heads, and other parts of their bodies; which makes the company of those that do so very savoury and sweet.

The Travels of Sig. Pietro della Valle, a Noble Roman in East-India and Arabia Deserta (1665) which includes passages written as letters home, describes the flowers he saw in India:

I saw a Canella, or Cinamon Tree, of which some are found in Goa, but stranger. 'Tis as big a Tree as any, not a shrub as I imagin'd; some of the leaves, which have a taste of Cinamon, and are pleasant to be masticated, I keep among my baggage to shew the same in Italy; as also some of the Tree Trisoe with its odiferous Flowers, which blow every day and night, and fall at the approach of day, as I my self saw and oberv'd of one that was planted before the Gate of our House. This Flower is very like the Jasmin of Catalonia, but the Canella hath a yellow one, which is us'd by the Country-people instead of Saffron with their meats, and upon other occasions. Moreover, I saw and observ'd in the Lake two sorts of Flowers, one great, the other very small, both white, with something of yellow in the midst; the lesser hath no green leaves on the stalk to be seen, and the inner part of the white leaves is full of thick long Doun: The greater flower hath smooth, long, and strait leaves, and grows on a Plant whose leaves are large, and almost perfectly round, swimming on the surface of the water, totally expanded almost like those of a Gourd. Both these Flowers have a strange property; in the night they are always clos'd, in the day always open, displaying themselves at the rising, and closing at the setting of the Sun; besides that they are of a very excellent fragrant smell... and tell a Fable of Brahma's being born of one of these Flowers, and afterwards re-entring into one again, wherein he hath spent ten thousand years. You see what fine Stories we have here; I leave them with you and kiss your Hands.

Japan – punishments

Not all the new cultural experiences of the travellers inspired awe; some were rather more gruesome. In *The Voyage of John Saris to Japan* (1613) the writer describes the fate of some prisoners:

> *When wee approached any Towne, we saw Crosses with the dead bodies of those who had been crucified thereupon; for crucifying is heere an ordinarie punishment for most Malefactors. Comming neere Surunga, where the Emperours Court is, wee saw a Scaffold with the heads of divers Crosses with the dead Corpses of those which had been executed remayning still upon them, and the pieces of other, which after their Executions had been hewen againe by the triall of others Cattans [Katana, a Japanese sword]. All which caused a most unsavourie passage to us, that to enter into Surunga must needs passe by them.*

North Africa – affable Arabs

The Adventures of Mr T. S. an English Merchant Taken Prisoner by the Turks of Algiers (1670) describes the Arabs he encountered in North Africa:

> *I saw here nothing of that rudeness, which our People imagine to be in all the Parts of Africa: The Place, and Attendance of the Prince, had as much of State and Glory, as is usual amongst the little Princes of Europe. I found nothing barbarous but their Language, which I could not well understand.*
>
>
>
> *The Arabs all about Africa are People very polite, and well bred; they have nothing of that baseness and uncivil carriage, which other more remote Nations have: They are imperious amongst the People that they have Conquered, because otherwise they could never retain them*

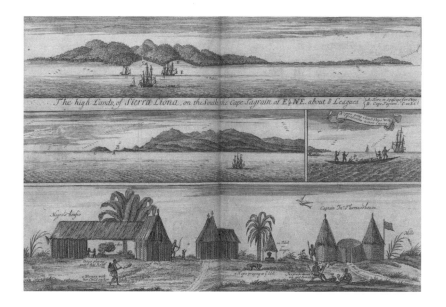

*in subjection to their Empire; but to Strangers that come amongst them,
they are affable, hospitable, courteous, kind, and very liberal.*

Sierra Leone – land of abundance

Portuguese sailors first landed in Sierra Leone on Africa's western
coast in the fifteenth century. Sierra Leone was one of the few countries in this wave-lashed area to have a safe harbour and so Freetown
became a popular trading post and a gateway to West Africa.

Dutch adventurer John Struys recorded his impressions of Sierra
Leone in *The Voyages and Travels of John Struys* (1684):

*Sierra Liones both in regard of its' Copiousness of Fruit, and Plenty
of Good Water is a very proper place to put in at, for Refreshment.
It abounds with Millets, Oranges, Lemmons, Banans, Cocos, Wild
Grapes, and abundance of many other sorts of Fruits; as also Sugar
canes and a kind of Long Pepper. It affoards, beside fruit-trees, good*

Timber, and Ingredients very useful in Dying.

The Inhabitants are not altogether black but tawny; and their bodies cauterized in many places with hot Irons. The tips of their Ears, and their noses, are bored through, and hung with Jewels, which they hold for passing rare Ornaments. Both Men and Women go naked, and use no manner of vesture save only a surcingle [belt], or towel; made of the barks of the Trees, which (it seems) for modesty sake, they wear about their Middle. Those that inhabit those parts which lie further within Land, are Cannibals (or Men-eaters) but such as dwell near the Sea, more civiliz'd and flexible to commerce with Europeans, and other Strangers.

Japan – the people

Portuguese Fernão Mendes Pinto was the first European to set foot in Japan in 1542, soon followed by a number of Jesuit missionaries. Japan was traditionally a very insular culture and the evangelistic zeal of the visiting Christians was seen as an unwelcome intrusion, so much so that in 1633 the shogun introduced a policy of *sakoku* (which translates as 'locked country') which meant that no foreigner could enter Japan and no Japanese could leave. The policy stayed in place until 1853.

Sakoku did not completely prevent all trade, but trade with the Europeans was only allowed through the Dutch East India Company warehouses in the port of Dejima in Nagasaki. This meant that Europe could still benefit from Japanese products but the people and culture remained mostly unknown to Europeans.

One of the few travellers to enter the country during this period was Dutchman John Struys. The account of his adventures *The Voyages and Travels of John Struys* (1684) has the following observations on the people of Japan:

The Japoneezes are reasonable fair of complexion, but a little more swarthy than Europeans. The ordinary Habit of the Man is not much distinguished from that of the Woman. They go all with long Robes thrown carelessly about their body, and tied round the middle with a Surcingle [belt]. The Ladies of the best quality, wear a garment of cloth of Gold and Silver, and that very richly embroidered. Their hair is neatly adorned with gems and precious stones. The men are robust and very personable; their Heads something duly bigger than is duly analogical with their Bodies. The Women are but slender, yet let their Body grow as it will, by wearing always a loose Garment, only their feet they screw and pinch as much as they can to make them little, which they think handsom: So that when they come to their full growth, have feet like Children of 5 or 6 years old.[29]

The Arctic – swarming profusion of life

Exploration of the northern Polar region was fraught with dangers as the severe cold and perilous conditions made travel there very difficult. The search for a Northwest Passage began at the end of the fifteenth century when John Cabot attempted to find a route through the Atlantic and Arctic Oceans to the Pacific. The sea ice prevented these early explorers from getting further than Newfoundland in Canada.

With stronger ships and better technology the search for the Northwest Passage really took off again in the nineteenth century and polar exploration captured the imagination of the general public

---

29 This seems to be a reference to the Chinese tradition of foot binding, which was not practised by the Japanese. It is possible that Struys had heard of the tradition in China and assumed it was also carried out in Japan.

as the quest to be the first to reach the North Pole intensified.

Discovery and Adventure in the Polar Seas and Regions by Professor Leslie, Professor Jameson and Hugh Murray (1844) contains this charming musing on the nature of the Polar region:

When we contemplate the aspect of the northern world, – bleak, naked, dreary, beaten by the raging tempest, and subject to an extremity of cold which, with us, is fatal to life and to all by which life is supported, – we naturally imagine that animal nature must exist there on a small scale, and under diminutive forms. It might be expected, that only a few dwarf and stunted species would be scattered along its melancholy shores, and that life, as it attempted to penetrate these realms of desolation, would grow faint and expire. But the mighty Architect of nature, whose ways and power far surpass human comprehension makes here a full display

*of his inexhaustible resources. He has filled these naked rocks and wintry
seas with a swarming profusion of life, such as he scarcely brings forth
under the most genial glow of tropical suns.*

Norwegian explorer Roald Amundsen became the first person to
sail the Northwest Passage in 1906 and the North Pole was supposedly reached by American Robert Peary in 1909 – although modern
experts now think he probably didn't reach the actual geographic
pole due to discrepancies in his record keeping. Roald Amundsen
was the first to have his journey to the Pole verified in 1926.

Panama – impenetrable jungle

Six Weeks in South America by E. H. S. (1850) is a relatively modern
work compared with some of the other accounts of exploration
contained in this book. This description of Panama is so evocative,
and the author even then was so appreciative of how much easier
his experience of Panama was compared to those pioneering early
explorers, it seems worthy of inclusion:

*The muddy banks actually steamed like a kettle set to boil, giving no
very favourable idea of the salubrity of the climate: bull-frogs croaked
in the thousands from the bush, caymen, half buried in ooze, slid lazily
into the river as we approached; while myriads of rainbow-coloured
birds and insects hovered among the overhanging branches, or perched
on clusters of equally brilliant flowers. I especially noticed a gigantic
butterfly, of which one specimen which we secured measured five inches
from wing to wing, and whose deep blue colour would have defied all the
artificial dyes of the painter's pallet to imitate its brightness. The under
part of the insect being a light dusky grey, almost devoid of colour, and
quite undistinguishable at the distance of a few paces from the bough
on which it lighted, the sudden way in which the creature appeared and
vanished again, added not a little to its picturesque effect.*

As to entomology, if it is any comfort to the traveller, when suffering under the persecutions of his winged tormentors, to know that he is being eaten at one and the same time by half a dozen undescribed species of insects, he may easily satisfy himself that his consolation is well founded; diminutive red fleas, ticks, and countless mosquitoes, he will probably recognize as familiar friends, and bear with accordingly. Notwithstanding these drawbacks from the pleasures of savage life, and the more serious annoyance of centipedes, tarantulas, and venomous spiders of Brobdignag dimensions, I often attempted to make my way into the recesses of the woods; but the difficulties of the undertaking always drove me back after proceeding a few hundred yards; and when panting with heat and hard work, and with clothes torn in a hundred places by the string hooked thorns of the underwood, I succeeded in regaining the path, it was impossible not to think, with astonishment and admiration, of the powers of endurance displayed by those early explorers, who, without guides, ignorant of the road, scantily provided with food and water, and continually exposed to the attacks of Indian tribes, then more numerous and fierce than now, struggled on through all difficulties to that unknown ocean, on whose shores they vainly expected to found an empire as enduring as their names.

Russia – the Tatars

The Tatars (formerly known as Tartars) are Turkic peoples living across Mongolia and modern-day Russia. *The True Travels, Adventures and Observations of Capitaine John Smith, in Europe, Asia, Africa, and America 1593–1629* (1630) includes the following description of the Tatar people:

The better sort are attired like Turks, but the plaine Tartar hath a blacke

sheepe skinne over his backe, and two of the legs tied about his necke, the other two about his middle, with another over his belly, and the legs tied in the like manner behinde him: then two more made like a pair of bases, serveth him for breeches; with a little close cap to his skull of blacke felt, and they use exceeding much of this felt, for carpets, for bedding, for Coat, and Idols.

Though the ground be fertile, they sow little corne, yet the Gentlemen have bread and hony-wine; grapes they have plenty, and wine privately, and good flesh and fish; but the common sort stamped millit, mingled alike with milke and water.

India – acrobats

British merchant Peter Mundy marvelled at the skilled Indian acrobats he observed performing in India, in *The Travels of Peter Mundy in Europe and Asia 1608–1667* (1667):

Towards night came Bazighurres, Men that use dauncinge, tumblinge, etts, Feats. And this among the rest. One Takes a pole of about three yards longe, which hee setteth upright upon his head, holdinge it with his hands, while a boye clambers up to the Topp of it (where is fastned a board halfe a foote broad) and with his feete stands upon it, when the other, lettinge goe his hold, daunceth about with him. More then that, the Boy Stood with his head on the said board with his heeles bolt upright in the Ayer, while the other daunceth with him as aforesaid, not once touching the pole with his hands.

Another tyme I sawe one sitting on the ground with his leggs a Crosse after this Countrie manner, then poyzeinge himselfe on his hands, hee brought upp his body backward very leasurely by degrees without touching the ground till it came over his head, his leggs remaininge in the same posture. Theis twoe Tricks mee thought were somewhat strange.

Japan – Osaka

John Saris was captain of the first English boat to reach Japan on a trade mission. *The Voyage of John Saris to Japan* (1613) has a description of the great Japanese city of Osaka:

> *We found Osaca to be a very great Towne, as great as London within the walls, with many faire Timber bridges of a great height, serving to passe over a river there as wide as the Thames at London. Some faire houses we found there, but not many. It is one of the chiefe Seaports of all Japan; having a Castle in it, marvellous large and strong, with very deepe trenches about it, and many draw bridges, with gates plated with yron. The Castle[30] is built all of Free-stone, with Bulwarks and Battlements, with loope holes for small shot and arrowes, and divers passages for to cast stones upon the assaylants. The walls are at least sixe or seven yards thicke, all (as I said) of Free-stone, without any filling in the inward part with trumpery, as they reported unto me. The stones are great, of excellent quarry, and are cut so exactly to fit the place where they are laid, that no morter is used, but onely earth cast betweene to fill up voyds crevises if any be.*

Mongolia – dwellings

The Mongol Empire was at its height in the twelfth and thirteenth centuries after Genghis Khan united the many nomadic tribes, ultimately creating the largest ever contiguous empire. In 1253 the Flemish monk William of Rubruck journeyed to the Mongol Empire as a missionary. He was one of the first Europeans to describe the Mongol culture and spent three years travelling throughout the Empire.

---

30 Work started on Osaka Castle in 1583 and it was complete by 1597, about 15 years before Saris's arrival. The castle still stands today, having been restored many times over its lifetime.

The nomadic lifestyle of Mongolians is described in *The Journey to the Eastern Parts of the World by Friar William of Rubruck 1253–55:*

Nowhere have they fixed dwelling-places, nor do they know where their next will be. They have divided among themselves Cithia [Scythia], which extendeth from the Danube to the rising of the sun; and every captain, according as he hath more or less men under him, knows the limits of his pasture lands and where to graze in winter and summer, spring and autumn. For in winter they go down to warmer regions in the south: in summer they go up to cooler towards the north. The pasture lands without water they graze over in winter when there is snow there, for the snow serveth them as water. They set up the dwelling in which they sleep on a circular frame of interlaced sticks converging into a little round hoop on the top, from which projects above a collar as a chimney, and this they cover over with white felt. Frequently they coat the felt with chalk, or white clay, or powdered bone, to make it appear whiter, and sometimes also black. The felt around this collar on top they decorate with various pretty designs. Before the entry they also suspend felt ornamented with various embroidered designs in color. For they embroider the felt, colored or otherwise, making vines and trees, birds and beasts.

And they make these houses so large they are sometimes thirty feet in width ... Furthermore they weave light twigs into squares of the size of a large chest, and over it from one end to the other they put a turtle-back also of twigs, and in the front end they make a little doorway; and then they cover this coffer or little house with black felt coated with tallow or ewe's milk, so that the rain cannot penetrate it, and they decorate it likewise with

embroidery work. And in such coffers they put all their bedding and valuables, and they tie them tightly on high carts drawn by camels, so that they can cross rivers.

When they set down their dwelling-houses, they always turn the door to the south, and after that they place the carts with coffers on either side near the house at a half stone's throw, so that the dwelling stands between two rows of carts, as between two walls.

Jamaica – the intolerable heat

A Short Journey in the West Indies in which are Interspersed Curious Anecdotes and Characters (1790) includes this somewhat melodramatic account of the climate of Jamaica, which conjures a rather evocative image of the poor sweaty author:

I now write to you from Jamaica ... The heat becomes intolerable. –Oh! For a glass of rasp-berry ice! – I am melting away – The sun is exhaling all my juices – I feel them passing through my pores. It is now the hottest time of the day – seven o'clock has struck, and the sun has been up for more than an hour. An extreme heat pervades the atmosphere, unfanned by the smallest breeze. The slightest action throws one into a violent perspiration.

Ceylon – the people

The Portuguese were the first Europeans to visit Sri Lanka in 1505 and set up a number of trading stations, but by 1638 the Dutch had secured a treaty to gain a monopoly of trade on the island. The Dutch rule held until 1802 when they ceded control to Britain and Sri Lanka became a crown colony.

In *Francois Valentijn's Descriptions of Ceylon* (1724) the Dutch minister and naturalist describes the people of Ceylon (Sri Lanka):

As regards the Cingalese, the native and oldest inhabitants of this land, they are not entirely black but brownish-yellow in colour, with long and wide ears, not large of stature, somewhat thin in the back, very weak of limbs, swift in body and very ingenious in mind, as they know how to make many beautiful things. They are very hardy by nature both in enduring many discomforts and in subsisting on poor food and little sleep.

As regards their nature and character, they are very friendly, and very much attached to their language. But they are also very greatly conceited and very proud, to such an extent that they will eat no food prepared in a house of one of lower rank than they imagine themselves to be, nor will they ever marry with them. Lying is not a sin nor a shame among them but a natural thing and they will not blanch the slightest when caught at it.

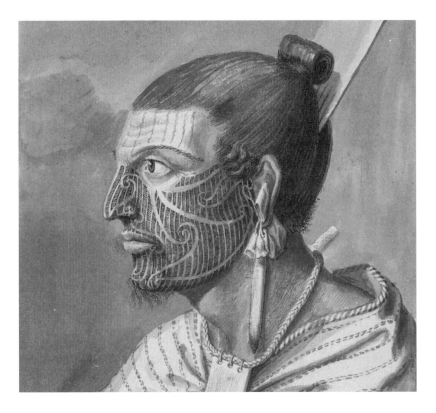

Valentijn goes on to discuss the everyday dress of the inhabitants of Ceylon:

The attire of the Cingalese, who generally have long smooth hair and thick beard like the Swiss, consists of a piece of cloth made into a jacket with folds or a cotton baju or a cloth that they wrap around their middle, pull through under the legs and let it hang down to the feet. On their heads they wear a red cap or cover it with something else. They decorate their ears with gold rings or jewels and they carry daggers on the side which are decorated with gold, silver and ivory handles.

The women wear a poor white skirt which is stitched with blue or red flowers and hangs down to the knee or somewhat lower, according to their high or low status. There is great difference between them. They also wear many silver arm rings and also many silver rings on the fingers and toes, silver necklaces, chains with stones, and also silver and gold rings and other trinkets on their bored ears.

The Pacific islands – tattoos

Although historically mostly associated with the Pacific islands, tattooing is actually surprisingly prevalent in the archaeological record around the world. China, India, Egypt, Japan, South America and even Europe[31] have all provided evidence of tattooing, mainly through the discovery of mummified bodies.

In Europe tattooing became synonymous with pagan beliefs and so as Christianity grew traditional pagan tattoos were suppressed. Captain Cook observed tattooed people in Tahiti, writing in *An Abridgement of Captain Cook's First and Second Voyages* (1788):

They stain their bodies, by indenting or pricking the flesh with a small instrument made of bone, cut into short teeth; which indentures they fill

---

31 The body of Otzi the Iceman from the 4th millennium BC found frozen in the ice of the Alps had a large number of small carbon tattoos.

with a dark blue or blackish mixture, prepared from the smoke of an oily nut, burnt by them instead of candles, and water; this operation, which is called by the natives Tattaowing; is exceedingly painful, and leaves an indelible mark on the skin. It is usually performed when they are about ten or twelve years of age, and on different parts of the body but those which suffer most severely are the breech and the loins, which are marked with arches, carried one above another a considerable way up their backs.

In *Narrative of a Voyage to the Pacific and Beerings Strait* (1831) Captain F. W. Beechey (1796–1856) wrote of the tattooing practices in the Easter Islands:

Tattooing or puncturing the skin is here practised to a greater extent than formerly, especially by the females, who have stained their skin in imitation of blue breeches:[32] copied no doubt, from some of their visiters, who frequently tuck up their trowsers to the knee in passing through the water. The deception, which, at short distance, completely deceives the eye, is produced by a succession of small blue lines, beginning at the waist and extending downward to the knee.

China – a tall story

Some of the explanations given for the things which the travellers did not understand are amazing, but it is little surprising that early explorers might accept the word of their hosts, especially considering many of the animals, plants and cultures they had recently encountered may have appeared equally improbable to them.

Here William of Rubruck (in *The Journey to the Eastern Parts of the World by Friar William of Rubruck 1253–55)* is told a tall tale of

---

32 Beechey here overestimates the influence of overseas 'visitors' on the tattooing practice of the inhabitants of the Easter Islands; it had in fact long been the tradition for islanders to tattoo a series of thin lines across their legs, which meant that to European eyes looking from a distance the person appears to be wearing trousers.

the provenance of a vibrant red dye (it is interesting to note that he appears to believe the first story, but doubts the second):

One day a priest from Cathay was seated with me, and he was dressed in a red stuff of the finest hue, and I asked whence he came such a colour; and he told me that in the countries east of Cathay there are high rocks, among which dwell creatures who have in all respects human forms, except that their knees do not bend, so that they get along by some kind of jumping motion; and they are not over a cubit in length, and all their little body is covered with hair, and they live in inaccessible caverns. And the hunters go carrying with them mead, with which they can bring on great drunkeness, and they make cup-like holes in the rocks, and fill them with this mead. So the hunters hide themselves and these animals come out of their caverns and taste this liquor, and cry "Chin, chin," so they have been given a name from this cry, and are called Chinchin. They then come in great numbers, and drink this mead, and get drunk and fall asleep. Then come the hunters, who bind the sleepers' feet and hands. After that they open a vein in their necks, and take out three or four drops of blood, and let them go free; and this blood he told me was most precious for colouring purples. They also told me as a fact (which I do not, however, believe), that there is a province beyond Cathay, and at whatever age a man enters it, that age he keeps which he had on entering.

Cape of Good Hope – the people

The Embassy of Sir Thomas Roe to the Court of the Great Mogul 1615–1619 contains this extremely disdainful impression of the people of South Africa who Sir Thomas Roe observed when he stopped at the Cape of Good Hope:

There is on the Island 5 or 600 people, the most barberous in the world, eating Carrione, wearing the gutts of sheepe about their Neckes for health, and rubbing their heads (curled like Negroos) with dung of beasts

and durte. They have noe other Cloathing then beastes skins wrapt on
their shoulders, the skinne next the body in heate, in cold the hairy syde.

China – abundant exports

The purpose of much of the travel in the Age of Exploration was to create trading routes and identify which commodities could be exploited. Here is a very telling observation from *Travels of Fray Sebastien Manrique 1629–1643* on the variety of items imported by the Portuguese, an account which would not seem out of place today over 350 years later:

> *The chief articles imported by the Portuguese from Southern India are a large amount of worked silks, such as Brocades, Brocatelles, Cloth Velvets, Damasks, Satins, Taffetas, Taffisirias, and Escomillas or Muslins, all from China. These were in every variety of colour, black excepted, which these people look upon as unlucky, only some fakirs using it to show their contempt for the world. The Portuguese bring also from China great quantities of porcelain, and many kinds of gilt articles such as bedsteads, tables, boxes, chests, writing-desks, as well as many other curios, of which there are large numbers in China. They also bring pearls and jewels of great value set in European style, but made with greater skill and more cheaply, as labour is very cheap in that great Empire of China, owing to the large number of workmen.*

Mongolia – divination

Flemish missionary William of Rubruck observed a Mongolian method of divination or scapulimancy in *The Journey to the Eastern Parts of the World by Friar William of Rubruck 1253–55*:

> *And as we were entering a servant came out carrying some sheep's shoulder-blades, burnt to coals, and I wondered greatly what he could do*

with them. When later on I enquired about it, I learnt that he does nothing in the world without first consulting these bones; he does not even allow a person to enter his dwelling without first consulting them. This kind of divination is done as follows: when he wishes to do anything, he has brought him three of these bones not previously charred, and holding one, he thinks of the thing about which he wishes to consult it, whether he shall do it or not; and then he hands it to a servant to burn. And there are two little buildings beside the dwelling in which he lives, in which they burn these bones, and these bones are looked for diligently every day throughout the whole camp. When they have been charred black, they are brought back to him, and then he examines whether the bones have been split by the heat throughout their length. In that case the way is open for him to act. If, however, the bones have been cracked crosswise, or round bits have started out of them, then he may not act. For this bone always splits in the fire, or there appear some cracks spreading over it. And if out of the three he finds one satisfactory, he acts.

Bangladesh – the people

In these days of globalisation people tend to dress in a fairly uniform fashion, only turning to traditional dress for special occasions. Differences in dress, jewellery and fashions must have been so much more marked in the seventeenth century when Portuguese Sebastien Manrique travelled across Asia. Here he discusses the clothing of the people of Bangladesh (*Travels of Fray Sebastien Manrique 1629–1643*):

The native of Bengala is of a medium dark colour; many even are black like the Chingalas of Ceylon. They are well featured and well formed in all their members, and are of moderate height. The common people, both men and women, wear cotton cloth, unshaped and unsewn. The men dress in cloth of six to seven handbreadths, worn from the waist downwards; above they are naked, and they also wear no shoes. They wear on the head a turban of from twelve to fourteen spans long and two

wide ... The women wear the same kind of cloth but in greater quantity,
usually from eighteen to twenty spans, with which they completely cover
the body ... The women usually have their arms covered with armlets or
bracelets, which latter differ in size and pattern from the armlets. These
rings are worn on the upper, central, and lower arm, so that the armlets
may strike the eye better: they also wear large rings in the ears and other
similar ornaments. In the walls of the nostrils, especially in the left wall,
they carry a tiny ring of gold or silver; a few, who can afford it, adding
one or two valuable pearls to it.

The superior attitude of Europeans towards other cultures
pervaded much of the writing of early explorers. Here it seems
Manrique is attempting to justify colonisation and slavery:

The Bengalas are a languid race and pusillanimous, given up, as
most Asiatic peoples are, to self-interest. The Bengalas are, therefore,
mean-spirited and cowardly, more apt to serve than to command, and
hence they easily accustom themselves to captivity and slavery. To
be well and successfully served by them they should be treated rather
with harshness than mildness; indeed this is so true that they have
a very common saying, Mare Tacūr, na mare Cucūr, which means
in our tongue, "He who chastises is Lord, he who does not is a cur".
From this the curious Reader can form an opinion as to the nature of
this people.

Java – teeth blackening

Teeth blackening has been a tradition across Southeast Asia since
prehistoric times. It was thought that only demons and wild animals
had perfect white teeth and so tooth blackening became a way of
showing superiority.

The World in Miniature (1824) by Frederic Shoberl (1775–1853)
contains this description of tooth blackening from the island of Java
in Indonesia:

Of the extravagant practices to which the Indian islanders have recourse with a view to improve the natural beauty of the human form, the most remarkable and universal is that of grinding and blackening the teeth. This operation is deemed so necessary a prelude to marriage, that when these people would inform you that a girl has arrived at the age of puberty, the common expression is: "She has had her teeth filed." It is chiefly confined to the upper canine teeth, the edges of which are made perfectly even, while the body of the tooth is rendered concave. The process which is tedious and rather painful, is performed by an old woman, who, while the patient lies on his back, grinds the teeth into the desired form with a bit of pumice-stone. After the loss of the enamel, an indelible black is easily given by the application of an oily carbon obtained from burnt cocoanut shell. The two upper front teeth are left white, and sometimes covered with a plate of gold: the contrast which they form in either case with the jet-black of their neighbours being considered as highly becoming. A few persons more whimsical than the generality, have the teeth filed into the appearance of a saw ... Habit has rendered this practice so familiar, that black teeth are looked upon as a real beauty, and white ones, which they would otherwise possess in perfection, are held in disesteem.

Easter Islands – mysterious monoliths

The Easter Islands are extremely remote, nestling as they do 2,300 miles west of South America and 1,100 miles from their nearest neighbouring island. It is thought these remote islands were settled in about AD 800 by Polynesians who would have had to negotiate hundreds of miles of open ocean in their outrigger canoes to reach land. These settlers (Rapa Nui), so cut off from their original ancestors, soon developed a distinct culture.

The iconic statues of Easter Island (known as moai) are still somewhat of a mystery to researchers, estimates for the date of their creation ranging from the tenth to sixteenth centuries. What is known is that they were hewn from local rock and somehow moved to stand on platforms overlooking the island, perhaps to represent benign ancestors or former chiefs.

In total there are 887 statues of varying sizes – some reach over 10 metres in height and weigh up to 86 tons. Almost half of the statues were found in the quarry where they were made but the rest were originally placed on stone platforms (ahu) mainly around the coast. Some statues had cylinders of red stone upon the head to represent the topknots traditionally worn by the Rapa Nui.

When first discovered the statues were thought to be just heads because the statues standing on the slopes of the volcano had been buried up to their shoulders by silt. Recent excavations have revealed the full size of the statues and uncovered carved 'tattoos' on the back of the monoliths.

The first Europeans to reach Easter Island were the Dutch, who first spotted the islands on Easter Sunday, 1722; hence the name. Dutch explorer Jacob Roggeveen (1659–1729) encountered a population already in crisis. Erosion caused by the deforestation of the island by the Rapa Nui people (possibly to make way for farmland or for setting fires) meant that they had no trees with which to make canoes so could not go fishing. *The Official Log of the Voyage of Mynheer Jacob Roggeveen* (1722) contains the first European description of the great monoliths:

What form of worship of these people comprises we were not able to gather any full knowledge of, owing to the shortness of our stay among them; we noticed only that they kindle fire in front of certain remarkable tall stone figures they set up; and, thereafter squatting on their heels with heads bowed down, they bring the palms of their hands together and alternately raise and lower them. At first, these stone figures caused us to be filled with wonder, for we could not understand how it was possible that people who are destitute of heavy or thick timber, and also of stout cordage, out of which to construct gear, had been able to erect them; nevertheless some of these statues were a good 30 feet in height and broad in proportion. This perplexity ceased, however, with the discovery on removing a piece of the stone, that they were formed out of clay or

some kind of rich earth, and that small smooth flints had been stuck over afterwards, which are fitted very closely and neatly to each other, so as to make up the semblance of a human figure.

Roggeveen's assumptions about the making of the statues were incorrect. The majority of the statues were carved from tuff, a compressed volcanic ash, quarried on the islands. By the time Captain Cook reached the Easter Islands in 1774 many of the moai had been toppled, according to *An Abridgement of Captain Cook's First and Second Voyages* (1788):

On the East side, near the sea, they met with three platforms of stone-work, or rather the ruins of them. – On each had stood four of those large statues, but they were all fallen down from two of them, and also one from the third; all except one broken by the fall, or in some measure defaced. Mr. Wales measured this one, and found it to be fifteen feet in length, and six feet broad over the shoulders. Each statue had on its head a large cylindric stone of a red colour, wrought perfectly round. The one they measured, which was not by far the largest, was fifty-two inches high, and sixty-six in diameter.

Sadly between that first visit by Europeans in 1722 and 1868[33] all the statues were toppled. When Captain F. W. Beechey arrived in 1831 (*Narrative of a Voyage to the Pacific and Beerings Strait*) he remarked:

The gigantic busts which excited the surprise of the first visiters to the island, have suffered so much, either from the effects of time, or maltreatment of the natives, that the existence of any of them at present is questionable.

The Rapa Nui people were thought to have overturned the remaining statues during clan warfare as their civilisation collapsed. Not only were they pushed to starvation by the loss of the trees but they were further decimated by Peruvian raids on the island in which many Rapa Nui were taken into slavery. From the mid-nineteenth century missionaries arrived and the unfortunate remaining Rapa Nui soon lost their culture as tattoos, traditional clothing and artworks were banned. Chile annexed the island in 1888 and soon no pure-blood Rapa Nui remained.

Bangladesh – Chittagong

The city of Bengala (now Chittagong) in Bangladesh is vividly brought to life by Portuguese friar Sebastien Manrique in his account *Travels of Fray Sebastien Manrique 1629–1643*:

Many strange nations resort to this City on account of its vast trade and commerce in a great variety of commodities, which are produced in profusion in the rich and fertile lands of this region. These have raised the City to an eminence of wealth which is actually stupefying, espe-cially when one sees and considers the large quantities of money which

---

33 In 1868 British ship's surgeon John Linton Palmer arrived at the Easter Islands aboard the HMS Topaze and recorded that all the statues had been toppled. The crew took one of the smaller *moai*, known as *Hoa Hakananai'a* back to England, where it is still on display today at the British Museum.

lie principally in the houses of the Cataris [khatri – the trading class in India], in such quantity indeed that, being difficult to count, it used commonly to be weighed. I was informed also, that the indigenous population of this Gangetic emporium and its suburbs exceeded two hundred thousand, irrespective of visitors who come in great numbers from all parts. Some of these came on mercantile business in order to take advantage of the great facilities offered by the place ... Nor was one less astounded at the great profusion to be found there of every kind of useful article and every species of food which a human being could desire, especially in its numerous Bazares or markets.

These Provinces of Bengala are very extensive and are much frequented by foreigners, owing to the trade there, both in food-stuffs, as I have remarked before, as also in fine cloth. So extensive is the trade that over one hundred vessels are yearly loaded up in the ports of Bengala with only rice, sugar, fats, oils, wax, and other similar articles.

Most of the cloth is made of cotton and manufactured with a delicacy and propriety not met with elsewhere. The finest and richest muslins are produced in this country, from fifty to sixty yards long and seven to eight handbreadths wide, with borders of gold and silver or coloured silks. So fine, indeed, are these muslins that merchants place them in hollow bambus, about two spans long, and, thus secured, carry them throughout Corazane [Khurasan in Persia], Persia, Turkey, and many other countries.

The strange tale of 'Astrachan fruit'

The Voyages and Travels of John Struys (1684) is at times a fanciful account of the Dutch sailmaker's extensive travels. At one point Struys was enslaved by Tatars and it is during this time that he came across Astrakhan[34] skins and is told a rather unlikely tale as to their provenance:

---

34 Astrakhan is the tightly curled fleece of a newborn or fetal karakul lamb. The fleece was highly prized by the Tatars, who used it to make traditional hats and coats.

In this Heath, or Wilderness, called the step is a strange kind of Fruit found, named Baronez, or Barnitsch, from the Word Boran which is a lamb in the Russian Tongue because of its form and similitude, much resembling a sheep have Head, Feet and Tail, and what is more worth of Note, a skin of white shining Hair and soft as Silk. This Skin is held in great esteem by the Tartars and Russes, and sold for a good price, as I have paid my self sometimes 5 or 6 Roebels and doubled my money when I sold it again. One of those skins is to be seen at the House of Mr. John Swammerdam, in Amsterdam, a Gentleman famous for collection of the Rarities of Nature from every place of the World: but that if his he had from a Seaman that had been formerly a slave in China, where coming into a Wood, found of this Fruit, and bought as many Skins as made him a Coat. The descriptions he gave of them, did very much agree with what the Inhabitants of Astrachan informed me of them. It grows upon a low stalk about 2 foot and a half high, some higher, and is supported just at the Navel: the Head always hangs down as if it pastured, or fed, of the Grass, and when the grass decays it perishes, but this I ever look'd upon as ridiculous, altho the Inhabitants asserverated to me by many Oaths, that they have often out of curiousity made experience of that, by cutting away the Grass, upon which it instantly fades away. However what I might further add as to what they say of this Fruit, and what I my self believe in the wonderfull Operations of a secret Sympathy in nature. I shall rather keep to my self, than aver, or impose upon the Reader, what, I am sensible will be universally exploded for a Fable.

Syria – carrier pigeons

Ancient Romans and Greeks used pigeons to convey messages (Julius Caesar was said to have used pigeons to carry instructions to his soldiers during the conquest of Gaul and the Greeks supposedly sent news of winners at the Olympic Games via pigeon). The Persians, famed for their skill in bird training, had set up regular pigeon post routes in Baghdad by the twelfth century.

William Biddulph in *The Travels of Four Englishmen and a Preacher into Africa, Asia, Troy, Bythinia, Thracia, and to the Blacke Sea* (1612) was initially fascinated by the carrier pigeons he observed in Syria:

Betwixt Aleppo and Babylon, merchants travell often over the desart of Arabia, and every quarter of the yeare Caravans come from thence with many hundred camels laden with merchandise. And their custome hath been, and is still sometimes, when they have occasion to send some sudden newes from Babylon, to fasten some briefe writing to one of the wings of a Bagdat, or Babylonian pigeon, or about her necke, in such sort, that it may not hinder her flying, and to send her to bringe newes to Aleppo, which is at least ten daies journey off: which when I heard at the first, it seemed to me wonderful strange, and almost incredible: but after I understood how they traine them to it, the strangeness thereof was diminished.

It is not known exactly when carrier pigeons were first used in Europe but there is evidence that a pigeon brought the news of the British victory at Waterloo in 1815 and by 1860 the founder of Reuters News Agency, Paul Reuter had set up a relay of pigeons to take financial news between Brussels and Aachen.

India & Bangladesh – opium-eaters

Opium use originated in Mesopotamia around 3400 BC and from there spread to Egypt. Used for both medicinal and recreational purposes, the opium poppy became very popular and its use spread through the trading routes of the Silk Road, taking it into China.

Prior to the seventeenth century opium was generally made into a drink, which was far less potent than the later habit of smoking opium in a tobacco pipe. The *Travels of Fray Sebastien Manrique 1629–1643* contains this description of opium use in Bangladesh:

This country also produces a plant called *Anfion* resembling our hemp, though the seed is rather finer and it is sown afresh every year. When it is in flower it is called *Posto*. From this plant and its fruit a very bitter black extract is obtained, called by them *Anfion*, which is largely used by Orientals to assist in the gratification of lust and lewdness, by increasing their sexual power. It must, however, be taken in moderation, as if taken in large quantity it is very injurious. Those who are accustomed to it can, at most, take four or five pesos in weight. This *Anfion* mixed with any proportion of oil is a powerful poison. One of its properties is to make it impossible for any opium-eater addicted to this drug to pass a whole day without it, and, if by chance they are unable to procure some, they are like moribund persons until they obtain it. Each failure to procure it renders them weaker, so that if they fail to obtain it for three or four days, or, at most, six days, they die.

The Travels of Peter Mundy in Europe and Asia 1608–1667 (1667) includes an account of opium use in India:

> *There were also many feilds of Poppie of which they make opium, called heere aphim by this Countrie people, much used for many purposes. The seede thereof they putt on their bread, I meane of white poppye. Of the huskes they make a kinde of Beveredge called Post, steepeing them in water a while, and squeezeinge and strayinge out the liquor, they drinck it, which doth inebriate.*

It seems that both these explorers observed the negative effects of opium and perhaps for this reason did not try it themselves. English merchant sailor Thomas Bowery (1669–1713) was not quite so reserved when it came to experiencing cannabis in Bengal, India. Bowery and ten of his English friends sampled some, becoming the first Europeans to record getting high:

> *It soon took it's Operation Upon most of us, but merrily, Save upon two of our Number, who I Suppose feared it might doe them harme not being accustomed thereto. One of them Sat himselfe downe Upon the floore, and wept bitterly all the Afternoone; the Other terrified with feare did runne his head into a great Mortavan Jarre, and continued in the Posture 4 hours or more, 4 or 5 of the number lay upon the Carpets (that were Spread in the roome) highly Complimentinge each Other in high termes, each man fancyinge himselfe noe less than an Emperour. One was quarralsome and fought with one of the wooden Pillars of the Porch, untill he had left himselfe little Skin upon the knuckles of his fingers. My Selfe and one more Sat sweatinge for the Space of 3 hours in Exceedinge Measure.*

Illustration credits

All illustrations from the British Library's collections

p.6 *Mr John Nieuhoff's Remarkable Voyages & Travells into y best Provinces of West and East Indies*, 1744. 455.f.2.

p.10 A.Vosmaer, *Description d'un recueil exquis d'animaux rares, consistant en quadru-pèdes, oiseaux et sepents, des Indes Orientales et Occidentales, s'ayant trouvés ci-devant aux Ménageries appartenantes à... Monseigneur le Prince d'Orange-Nassau*, 1804. 7205.e.23.

p.13 Ulisse Aldrovandi, *Ornithologiae..libri XII*, 1646. 439.m.2-4.

p.16 Marie Sibylla Merian, *Dissertio de generatione et metamophosibus insectorum Surinamensium...*, 1726. 649.c.20.

p.18 *Beschryvinghe vande voyagie om den geheelen Werelt Cloot, ghedaen door O. van Noort...*, 1619. 983.ff.6.(11.).

p.21 Ulisse Aldrovandi, *De quadrupedibus solidipedibus...*, 1616. 459.b.6.(2.).

p.25 *A Collection of Drawings by A. Buchan, S. Parkinson and J.F. Miller, made in the Countries visited by Capt. Cook in his First Voyage, also of Prints published in Hawksworth's Voyages of Biron, Wallis and Cook, as well as in Cook's second and third voyages*, 1768-1780. Add. 23921, f.115r.

p.27 Theodore de Bry, *Decima tertia pars historiae Americanae...*, 1634. 566.l.9.(2.).

p.28 *A Collection of Voyages and Travels, etc.*, 1744. 455.f.2.

p.29 Mark Catesby, *The natural History of Carolina, Florida and the Bahama Islands*, 1731-43. 44.k.7-9.

p.30 Gonzalo Fernandez de Oviedo y Valdés, *La historia general de las Indias*, 1535. C.20.d.4.

p.35 Edward Topsell, *The History of Four-footed Beasts and Serpents...*, 1658. 37.f.22.

p.37 Athanasius Kircher, *China monumentis, quà sacris quà profanes, nec non variis naturae et artis spectaculis, aliarumque verum memorabilium argumentis illustrate, etc.*, 1667. 150.k.15.

p.39 Sir Thomas Herbert, *Some years travels into divers parts of Africa, and Asia the great*, 1677. 215.e.12.

p.40 Giovanni Francesco Gemelli Careri, *A Voyage round the world*, 1732. 455.f.4.

p.47 Pierre Belon, *De aquatilibus, libri duo*, 1553. 446.a.6.

p.50 Sir Thomas Herbert, *Some years travels into divers parts of Africa, and Asia the great*, 1677. 215.e.12.

p.59 *A Collection of Voyages and Travels, etc.*, 1744. 455.f.2.

p.62 Daniel Beeckman, *A Voyage to and from the Island of Borneo...*, 1718. 980.i.18.

p.63 Athanasius Kircher, *China monumentis, quà sacris quà profanes, nec non variis*

*naturae et artis spectaculis, aliarumque verum memorabilium argumentis illustrate,
etc.*, 1667. 150.k.15.

p.64 John Gabriel Stedman, *Narrative of a five years expedition against the revolted
Negroes of Surinam, from the year 1772 to 1777, elucidating the history of that country
and describing its productions*, 1796. 145.f.15.

p.66 *Journal kept on board the Minerva transport, from Ireland to New South Wales and
Bengal, by John Washington Price, Surgeon, May 1798-June 1800*. Add. 13880, f.86.

p.69 Jean Barbot, *...a new relation of the province of Guiana, and of the Great Rivers of
Amazons and Oronoque in South America*, 1746. 455.f.5.

p.70 *Drawn from the life, 1ˢᵗ June 1798, from one sent from Chittagong by Mr Crommelin.*
NHD 32, f.24.

p.72 Sebastian Münster, *Cosmographey*, 1578. 569.h.25.

p.75 *A Collection of Voyages and Travels, etc.*, 1744. 455.f.2.

p.76 Giovanni Francesco Gemelli Careri, *A Voyage round the world*, 1732. 455.f.4.

p.79 Pierre Belon, *L'histoire naturelle des estranges poisons marins,... & de plusiers autres
de son espece*, 1551.

p.80 Sir Thomas Herbert, *Some years travels into divers parts of Africa, and Asia the
great*, 1677. 215.e.12.

p.82 Albertus Seba, *Locupletissimi rerum naturalium thesauri accurate description*,
1734-65. 457.g.1-4.

p.84 f Conrad Gesner, *Historiae Animalium*, 1551. 460.c.6.

p.87 Isaac de la Peyrère, *An account of Greenland*, 1732. 455.f.2.

p.92 Francis Willughby, *The Ornithology of F.W. ...*, 1678. 438.m.6.

p.94 Jan Huygen van Linschoten, *Itinerario, voyage ofter Schipvaert...*, 1596. 569.g.23.

p.97 William Alexander, *The Costume of China*, 1805. 455.e.9.

p.101 Richard Ligon, *A True & Exact History of the Island of Barbados*, 1657. 147.d.10.

p.105 *A Collection of Voyages and Travels, etc.*, 1744. 455.f.2.

p.106 Giovanni Francesco Gemelli Careri, *A Voyage round the world*, 1732. 455.f.4.

p.108 Richard Ligon, *A True & Exact History of the Island of Barbados*, 1657. 147.d.10.

p.110 Sir Thomas Herbert, *Some years travels into divers parts of Africa, and Asia the
great*, 1677. 215.e.12.

p.115 Athanasius Kircher, *China monumentis, quà sacris quà profanes, nec non variis
naturae et artis spectaculis, aliarumque verum memorabilium argumentis illustrate,
etc.*, 1667. 150.k.15.

p.117 Richard Bridgens, *West India Scenery...*, 1836. 789.g.13.

p.120 Giovanni Francesco Gemelli Careri, *A Voyage round the world*, 1732. 455.f.4.

p. 125 *A Collection of Drawings by A. Buchan, S. Parkinson and J.F. Miller, made in
the Countries visited by Capt. Cook in his First Voyage, also of Prints published in
Hawksworth's Voyages of Biron, Wallis and Cook, as well as in Cook's second and third
voyages*, 1768-1780. Add. 23921, f.117r.

p.126 Marie Sibylla Merian, *Dissertio de generatione et metamophosibus insectorum
Surinamensium...*, 1726. 649.c.20.

p.128 *A Collection of Voyages and Travels, etc.*, 1744. 455.f.2.

p.129 Giovanni Francesco Gemelli Careri, *A Voyage round the world*, 1732. 455.f.4.

p.130 Richard Bridgens, *West India Scenery...*, 1836. 789.g.13.

p.133 *A Collection of Voyages and Travels, etc.*, 1744. 455.f.2.

p.139 Philippe Sylvestre Dufour, *Traitez nouveaux & curieux du café, du thé et du chocolate*, 1688. 449.a.6.

p.140 *Drawings in Indian ink, illustrative of Capt. Cook's first voyage, 1768-1770.* Add. 15508, f.15.

p.143 *Drawings in Indian ink, illustrative of Capt. Cook's first voyage, 1768-1770.* Add. 15508, f.10.

p.145 *An account of origins and occupations of some of the sects, castes and tribes of India. Written at Hansi Cantonment for Colonel James Skinner*, 1825. Add. 27255, f.267v.

p.149 Theodore de Bry, *Decima tertia pars historiae Americanae...* , 1634. 566.l.9.(2.).

p.151 Friedrich Ratzell, *The history of mankind*, 1896-98. 572*3343*.

p.152 *Hindu villagers at Puri in Orissa*, watercolour, 1820. WD 869.

p.154 James Cowles Prichard, *The Natural History of Man*, 1845. 10007.d.23.

p.159 Sydney Parkinson, *A Journal of a Voyage to the South Seas, in His Majesty's Ship, the Endeavour*, 1773. G.7422.

p.162 Évariste Régis Huc, *Souvenirs d'un Voyage dans la Tartarie et le Thibet*, 1854. 10056.d.22.

p.163 *A Collection of Voyages and Travels, etc.*, 1744. 455.f.2.

p.165 Arnoldus Montanus, *Atlas Japannensis, being remarkable addresses by way of embassy from the East-India Company of the United Provinces, to the Emperor of Japan...*, 1670.

p.166 *Collections of Costumes of Various Nations*, 18th century. Add. 5253, f.8.

p. 168 *Collections of Costumes of Various Nations*, 18th century. Add. 5253, f.56.

p.171 *A Collection of engravings, etchings and woodcuts of various sizes mainly illustrating the costumes of different nations*, 15th-17th centuries. 146.i.10.

p.173 *Drawings in Indian ink, illustrative of Capt. Cook's first voyage, 1768-1770.* Add. 15508, f.23.

p.182 *A Collection of Drawings by A. Buchan, S. Parkinson and J.F. Miller, made in the Countries visited by Capt. Cook in his First Voyage, also of Prints published in Hawksworth's Voyages of Biron, Wallis and Cook, as well as in Cook's second and third voyages*, 1768-1780. Add. 23921, f.64.

p.187 Auguste van Pers, *Nederlandsch Oost-Indischen Typen...*, 1854-56. 1781.c.23.

A huge thank you to my wonderful editor Jon Crabb for helping me to make the book the best it can be.

To Bryn, Soren and Romilly –
who help me find wonder in everything.

First published in 2016 by

The British Library
96 Euston Road
London NW1 2DB

Cataloguing in publication data

A catalogue record for this book is available
from the British Library

ISBN 978 0 7123 5636 7

Designed and typeset by
Briony Hartley, Goldust Design
Printed in Malta by Gutenberg Press